Changing Firm Boundaries in a New Information
and Communication Environment

European University Studies

Europäische Hochschulschriften
Publications Universitaires Européennes

Series V
Economics and Management

Reihe V Série V
Volks- und Betriebswirtschaft
Sciences économiques, gestion d'entreprise

Vol./Bd. 2996

PETER LANG

Frankfurt am Main · Berlin · Bern · Bruxelles · New York · Oxford · Wien

Christian Bender

Changing Firm Boundaries in a New Information and Communication Environment

Evidence from the Manufacturing and Music Industry

PETER LANG
Europäischer Verlag der Wissenschaften

Bibliographic Information published by Die Deutsche Bibliothek
Die Deutsche Bibliothek lists this publication in the Deutsche Nationalbibliografie; detailed bibliographic data is available in the internet at <http://dnb.ddb.de>.

Zugl.: Münster (Westfalen), Univ., Diss., 2002

Gedruckt auf alterungsbeständigem,
säurefreiem Papier.

D 6
ISSN 0531-7339
ISBN 3-631-51464-6
US-ISBN 0-8204-4694-5

© Peter Lang GmbH
Europäischer Verlag der Wissenschaften
Frankfurt am Main 2003
All rights reserved.

Printed in Germany 1 2 3 4 6 7

www.peterlang.de

Acknowledgements

The completion of this dissertation would not have been possible without the generous assistance of numerous people. I would like to take this chance to express my gratitude to everyone who has made it possible for me to successfully complete this project.

First, I would like to thank my advisor, Professor Christian Harm, for taking me as his Ph.D. student and giving me all the motivation, space for creativity, and guidance I needed in my research work. His influence was crucial for my academic performance. I would also like to thank Professor Stefan Klein for his advice and his role as a co-supervisor.

I also owe a debt of gratitude to the University of Muenster's International Business Department and its entire staff for providing a wonderful environment for research and helpful administrative support. In particular, I thank Georg Rindermann, Carsten Hahn, Thomas Roehling, Doris Hohmeier, Nicole Neunhoeffer and Torsten Engel for proofreading and comments. In addition, I would like to express my sincere appreciation for the people at the International Business Department, Stern School of Business, New York University, for their hospitality and inspiring discussions during my stay as a visiting doctoral student in 2001.

The funding from the German Academic Exchange Service (DAAD) has also been essential in supporting my research financially during my time as a visiting doctoral student at NYU. I also thank Alcatel SEL Stiftung für Kommunikationsforschung for awarding me their 2003 Dissertation Award. Finally, I thank my girlfriend Frauke and my parents for their understanding and encouragement.

Table of Contents

List of Figures

List of Tables

List of Abbreviations

A&R	Artist and Repertoire
APS	Advanced Planning Systems
bn	Billion
BMI	Broadcast Music Inc.
CD	Compact Disc
CORI	Contract and Organizational Research Institute
CPFR	Collaborative Planning, Forecasting and Replenishment Committee
DRM	Digital Rights Management
DVD	Digital Versatile Disc
EDI	Electronic Data Interchange
ERP	Enterprise Resource Planning
FB	Fisher Body
FE	Fixed Effects
FOC	First Order Condition
GDP	Gross Domestic Product
GEMA	Gesellschaft für musikalische Aufführungs- und mechanische Vervielfältigungsrechte
GM	General Motors
GV	Global Vantage
HTML	Hypertext Markup Language
ICT	Information and Communication Technology
IFPI	International Federation of the Phonographic Industry
IIS-A	Fraunhofer Institute for Integrated Circuits
IO	Industrial Organization
IOS	Interorganizational Information Systems
IP	Internet Protocol
IPR	Intellectual Property Rights
IT	Information Technology
ITU	International Telecommunication Union
JIT	Just-in-Time
LDC	Least Developed Countries

m	million
M&A	Mergers & Acquisitions
MP3	Motion Picture Expert Group Layer-3
MPEG	Motion Picture Expert Group
MVI	Manufacturing Vertical Integration
OB	Organizational Behavior
OECD	Organization for Economic Cooperation and Development
OEM	Original Equipment Manufacturer
OLS	Ordinary Least Squares
P2P	Peer-to-Peer
PC	Personal Computer
POLCON	Political Constraint
R&D	Research and Development
RE	Random Effects
RIAA	Recording Industry Association of America
SCM	Supply Chain Management
SIC Code	Standard Industrial Classification Code
TCE	Transaction Cost Economics
TRIPS	Trade-related Aspects of Intellectual Property Rights
TV	Television
TVI	Total Vertical Integration
US	United States of America
USD	United States Dollars
VAI	Value-added Index
VAP	Value-added Partnerships
VIC	Vertical Industry Connection
WCT	World Intellectual Property Organization Copyright Treaty
WIPO	World Intellectual Property Organization
WPPT	World Intellectual Property Organization Performances and Phonograms Treaty
WTO	World Trade Organization

Abstract

The nature of the firm has changed since COASE (1937) and the birth of the theory of the firm. An important change is the advent of modern information and communication technology (ICT) that altered the business environment. The objective of the dissertation is to study the transformation of corporate organization by analyzing the impact of a changing information and communication environment on firm boundaries. Therefore I study firm boundaries in the manufacturing and the media sector. These two sectors are selected to illustrate important differences in the change of firm boundaries. Although both showed an impact of ICT, the direction of this change has been different because of contrary product characteristics. The reason is that ICT in the manufacturing sector mainly leads to communication and coordination improvements, while it induces problems to protect intellectual property rights (IPRs) in the media sector.

In the first part the manufacturing sector is analyzed. Hypotheses regarding the impact of ICT on the governance of business activity are developed based on arguments from Transaction Cost Economics (TCE). I subsequently check these hypotheses against manufacturing industry data in a panel regression design. It is explored to what extent the international dissemination of ICT acted as a catalyst in changing organizational structures. Therefore I compare the degree of vertical integration of manufacturing firms in different countries over time and analyze the role of ICT in this context. The analysis is controlled for alternative determinants of firm boundaries including the institutional, economic and political environment. Vertical disintegration, i.e. slimmer firms, can be found particularly in business environments with high ICT penetration. This can be regarded as tentative evidence for ICT-triggered outsourcing.

The second part focuses on firm boundary changes in the media sector. Media firm boundaries appear to move in the opposite direction: recent increases in vertical integration by major media firms are analyzed regarding the impact of ICT. Using an eclectic theory synopsis, IPRs are identified as an important variable in the relationship between ICT and media firm boundaries. Hence, the impact of ICT on media firm boundaries is studied indirectly by looking at the connection between ICT and IPRs: I test the effect of ICT penetration on recorded music sales figures in a panel regression. The tests show a significant negative impact of ICT on music sales what can be interpreted as a loss of IPRs via ICT-enabled music piracy. Music firms loose sales in business environments with enhanced technological copying capabilities. I conjecture that vertical integration increases are a response of media firms to regain and maintain control over the production and distribution of their products. In addition, the effect of IPR protection is taken into account. Recent regulatory action in form of international treaties initiated by the World Intellectual Property Organization (WIPO) seems to contribute to contain IPR loss.

In my empirical analyses I find evidence that supports the view that the ICT shock has an ambivalent impact on firm boundaries. The comparison of the manufacturing and the media sector shows that distinct product characteristics like intangibility determine the direction of the ICT-induced shift in firm boundaries. ICT plays a role in the fragmentation of value-chains in the manufacturing sector but can provide vertical integration incentives in the media sector.

1. Introduction

Firm boundaries are in constant flux. Nowadays, the boundaries of the firm that Ronald Coase had in mind when he wrote his seminal paper on the nature of the firm[2] are not only changing but are increasingly difficult to identify.[3] Casual empiricism shows that outsourcing[4] and contract manufacturing has become a major trend in the manufacturing sector.

What started as an exception at IBM[5] in the 1980s became more and more popular in recent years. There are several cases of corporate reorganization that can be seen as examples for this trend. Swedish telecom equipment maker Ericsson outsourced nearly all of its handset manufacturing to Flextronics International Ltd. at the beginning of 2001. Comparable examples include Cisco that owns only three plants for its high-tech equipment and prototypes, Apple Computer that sold its largest PC plant in the US to SCI Systems in 1996, and Fujitsu Siemens Computers that contracted out its German network server production to Flextronics in January 2000.[6] The Canadian-based telecommunications and computer equipment firm Nortel Networks has outsourced manufacturing on a large scale in the last two years and reduced the degree of vertical integration into its suppliers by introducing e2open[7], an Internet business-to-business marketplace for the electronics industry with 60 potential suppliers.[8]

---

[1] SHAPIRO/VARIAN (1999), p. 1-2.
[2] See COASE (1937).
[3] COASE spent the academic year 1931/32 on a travelling scholarship in the United States studying the structure of US-American industries before writing the article for which he was awarded the Nobel Price in Economic Sciences in 1991, see COASE (1992).
[4] I understand outsourcing as an arrangement in which one company provides services for another company that could also be or usually have been provided in-house, i.e. it relies on a supplier contract for outside procurement instead of an employment contract for in-house production.
[5] IBM introduced the idea of outsourcing entire products in the 1980s by contracting out its personal computer manufacturing to SCI Systems Inc.
[6] See THE ECONOMIST (2000a).
[7] e2open is an electronic exchange for original equipment manufacturers (OEMs), contract manufacturers, distributors and suppliers in the electronics industry. e2open was formed by Acer, Hitachi, IBM, LG Electronics, Lucent Technologies, Matsushita Electric (Panasonic), Nortel Networks, Seagate Technology, Solectron and Toshiba. A comparable electronic exchange for the automotive sector is Covisint by Ford, GM, DaimlerChrysler and Renault/Nissan and some members of the metal industry.
[8] See THE ECONOMIST (2000a).

In 2000, Flextronics, Solectron, SCI Systems, Celestica, Jabil and hundreds of smaller contract firms owned 11% of the market for electronics hardware.[9] In a survey of US-American companies, 54% of the surveyed companies said that they have outsourced manufacturing processes or services in the past 2 to 3 years versus 38% who have done no new outsourcing. 46% of companies reported that they had increased their outsourcing activity over the past 2 to 3 years versus just 4% stating that they are moving in the opposite direction.[10]

The phenomenon is not restricted to the electronics manufacturing industry[11] even though the average electronics OEM outsourced 73% of its manufacturing.[12] Even General Motors (GM), traditionally a synonym for vertical integration, spun off Delphi Automotive Systems, one of its supply divisions.[13] Similarly, Ford Motor Company transformed its supply division, Visteon Automotive Systems, into a separate legal entity. GM had already spun-off its North American internal IT services provider Electronic Data Systems Corporation (EDS) in 1996. In 2001, roughly 2/3 of the North-American automobile industry's value (an estimated USD 750 billion) resides with suppliers.[14]

A sharp contrast to the vertical disintegration in the manufacturing sector takes place in the media sector. The bulk of already vertically integrated global media companies are increasing their vertical integration:[15] recent mergers and acquisitions, e.g. Vivendi-Universal and AOL-Time Warner, combine media content producers with distribution channels.

This dissertation analyzes the role information and communication technology (ICT) plays as a potential determinant of changes in vertical integration observed in the manufacturing and the media sector.

---

[9] See THE ECONOMIST (2000b).
[10] See PORTER (1999).
[11] The automotive industry is another example of casual empiricism that indicates a trend towards more outsourcing. For example, vertical integration for E- and S-type DaimlerChrysler models decreased from 50% to 38% during the 1990s. The manufacturing of A-type and Smart models has a degree of vertical integration of 30% and 20% respectively, see VERKEHRSBRIEF (2001).
[12] See DOIG ET AL (2001), p. 1.
[13] See THE ECONOMIST (2001a), p. 88. GM has a large amount of highly specialized inanimate assets, ranging from plant and machinery to world famous brand names, see RAJAN/ZINGALES (2000).
[14] See DOIG ET AL (2001), p. 1.
[15] See GARDINI (2002).

1.1   Research Idea and Motivation

What we observe in the manufacturing sector is a change in the nature of the firm that looks like a break-up of the old vertically integrated "Modern Business Enterprise"[16] in the sense of CHANDLER (1977). The epitome of vertical integration has been John D. Rockefeller's Standard Oil Trust that comprised the whole petroleum value-chain from exploration to distribution. Owning Amazon rubber trees and railroads Ford Motor Company represented a similar example in the 1920s.[17] The question is if this can be understood as partially replacing the visible hand of a hierarchy by the invisible hand of the market mechanism. ZINGALES (2000, p. 3) describes these changes as follows:

> *„Large conglomerates have been broken up, and their units have been spun off as stand-alone companies. Vertically integrated manufacturers have relinquished direct control of their suppliers and moved towards looser forms of collaboration. "*

Increasing usage of ICT has been reported to play an important role in enabling this outsourcing, e.g. via sharing data (e.g. inventory levels)[18] with upstream and downstream business partners or via ICT-enabled standardization and automatization of business processes.[19] An explanation that can be found for this pattern in the popular press[20] - but that is also popular among academics[21] - concludes that ICT has contributed to breaking up value-chains. Hence, ICT acted as a driver in the creation of smaller business entities. One aspect of this process is a potential vertical disintegration.[22]

AUDRETSCH (1995) notes that both Germany and the US saw massive size reductions in the corporate landscape in the early 1990s. This shrinking was triggered by the emergence of new ICT (electronic mail, shared databases etc.) that reduced the role of the traditional middle management whose original task was to channel information through the hierarchy.

---

[16] This term has been coined by CHANDLER (1977) to describe the prevalent form of business organization in the US. Prominent examples of these firms with enormous scale and scope are GM or Ford.
[17] See THE ECONOMIST (2001b), p. 16.
[18] Communicating inventory levels up- and downstream as a task to be performed by the supply chain management of a firm is supposed to be facilitated by ICT.
[19] See PICOT ET AL (2001), p. 72.
[20] See THE ECONOMIST (2000b).
[21] See e.g. BRYNJOLFSSON ET AL (1994).

The case examples just mentioned are not contradictory to the view that – among other enabling factors – ICT can provide the means for firms to outsource parts of their value chain, e.g. certain production stages. It thereby allows to separate different stages of a production process to be performed in various firms instead of producing everything in one entity. This can happen, for example, in the form of spinning-off an internal supplier and substituting this internal transaction with a supplier connected by EDI[23] or a business-to-business electronic commerce marketplace for procurement from (now external) and potentially multiple suppliers.

The thought that new technology has a substantial impact on firm organization is not entirely new. MILGROM/ROBERTS (1992) depict that the shift from handicraft production to mass-production was largely determined by three main technological innovations: steam ships, the railroad, and the telegraph. All three can be understood as long-distances means of coordination.[24] Nobel laureate James Buchanan sees the diffusion of ICT as having an impact on the important questions in economic and business research: "Who could question the critical importance of the information processing revolution in shaping the very questions that economists ask and attempt to answer?"[25]

Firms and markets have been modeled as information processing entities in the theoretical literature.[26] Thus, one might reasonably suspect that recent organizational change is related to variation in the ICT environment. Since the concept of the firm as an information processing entity is too vague, I will use a firm definition based on Transaction Cost Economics (TCE) logic.[27] However, the process of in- or outsourcing by virtue of ICT-related transaction cost reductions is still a hypothesized explanation for what we might perceive as 'moves-to-the-market' or 'moves-to-the-hierarchy'.

One way to make this hypothesized explanation observable for empirical research is to look at firm boundaries, in particular the degree of vertical integration, and compare it to the ICT-based external/market coordination mechanisms that are available for various firms at a

---

[22] See EVANS/WURSTER (1999).
[23] EDI stands for Electronic Data Interchange.
[24] See HITT (1998), p.1.
[25] BUCHANAN (1992), p. 21.
[26] See HAYEK (1945), ARROW (1973), and GALBRAITH (1977).
[27] See WILLIAMSON (1975, 1985).

certain time in different countries.[28] This cross-country view (to induce variance in the levels of ICT development and the institutional environment) has then to be extended by a longitudinal (temporal) dimension in order to gain information about the impact of change in the ICT environment on vertical integration.

Therefore, the central research question treated here is the question if the case examples used as casual empiricism in the beginning are really paradigmatic, i.e. if the potential break-up of the value-chain can be measured empirically. This issue is addressed by examining the following question: are shifts in the degree of vertical integration determined by changes in the ICT environment? Controlling for alternative determinants of change in firm boundaries pointing in the same direction and/or moderating the analyzed relationship direction and/or intensity is certainly indispensable but should be a feasible task.

The notion that ICT enables vertical disintegration is not necessarily an universal explanation for all industries. A look at the media sector adds an important facet to the research question. Casual empiricism shows that recent changes in media firm boundaries are targeted in a different direction compared to the manufacturing sector. In contrast to the manufacturing industry, media firm boundaries reveal an increase in vertical integration.[29] As shown later in the analysis the crucial reason for this difference is product intangibility in the media sector. For example, Rupert Murdoch's News Corporation currently owns a baseball team (Los Angeles Dodgers) and a movie studio (20th Century Fox) to produce contents for its broadcasting assets (Fox Television Channel).[30] The similarity to Ford Motor Company in the 1920s that owned its own rubber trees to manufacture the tires[31] for its cars is evident. Why do media firms draw firm boundaries that resemble manufacturing firms of the past? Again, ICT is supposed to be a main driver of this process and an important element of the answer to this question.

---

[28] Outsourcing IT, accounting or other functional organizational units is considered to be horizontal outsourcing. Here, we focus on vertical outsourcing activity that includes upstream (production of inputs) and downstream (marketing and distribution channel) parts of the value-chain.
[29] LEVENSTEIN (2002).
[30] See THE ECONOMIST (2002a): another example in the media sector is America Online (AOL), an Internet firm, that merged with Time Warner, a traditional media group, in early 2000. In June 2000, Vivendi, a French utilities group, merged with Seagram, owner of Universal Music, to form another vertically integrated media firm, Vivendi Universal. Vivendi Universal now controls assets from media content production to the distribution channels.
[31] See THE ECONOMIST (2001b), p. 16.

1.2   Proceeding and Results

My proceeding to analyze the research question we be as follows. First, I conduct a comprehensive review of the theoretical and empirical literature analyzing the impact of ICT on firm boundaries. This literature review includes a model by WILLIAMSON (1991) that is used to motivate the differences in the impact of ICT on firm boundaries between the manufacturing and the media sector. Then, I will provide evidence for the manufacturing sector (chapter three) and media sector (chapter four). I will focus on the manufacturing and the media sector because both sectors are affected by ICT-induced changes in firm boundaries, but in a different way.

Chapter one serves as an introduction to the research question that contains both, casual empiricism and theoretical reasoning to illustrate the research problem.

Chapter two contains a literature review of the related theoretical[32] and empirical contributions to the main topic. The synopsis comprises the theoretical and empirical literature on the determinants of firm boundaries in general and ICT impact on firm boundaries in particular. This allows an assessment of their explanatory power for variance in business organization. The TCE paradigm and some of its extensions are discussed critically in terms of suitability for the purpose of this analysis. TCE sees the firm as an alternative to the market mechanism to govern a transaction. I follow this approach and use a governance perspective to analyze the effects of ICT on firm boundaries. This perspective focuses ceteris paribus on the boundaries of the firm where firm and market meet as a transaction governance mechanism. Chapter two has the intention to clarify the missing piece of research by pursuing a comprehensive literature review and thereby indicate the point of departure for my own research contribution. The missing piece, i.e. the core of my own research contribution, is a comprehensive study of ICT as a determinant of the institutional environment in which transactions between and within firms take place. The final part of chapter two presents a

---

[32] Theoretical parts are contained in chapter two, three and four. In chapter two, theoretical contributions to the research question are summarized in order to define my own research question. The central piece of theory is a model by WILLIAMSON (1991) that is presented at the end of chapter two. Chapter three applies this model so that testable hypotheses can be derived. The additional theory added in chapter four (double marginalization, public good theory) is need to construct an eclectic theory framework to analyze effects that are idiosyncratic to the media sector.

simple heuristic governance model based on WILLIAMSON (1991) that is used to derive the hypothesis in the following chapter.

Chapter three contains the research design and empirical results for the manufacturing sector. Therefore, I show the ICT shock in the WILLIAMSON (1991) model portrayed in chapter two. These testable hypotheses are derived by operationalizing the theoretical outcome of this heuristic governance model in order to make it susceptible for an empirical analysis. I use firm balance sheet data taken from the Compustat Global Industrial/Commercial database to construct a value-added index as a proxy for vertical integration at the country-level that is compared in different ICT environments. Using this index I perform two main empirical analyses in this chapter: first, I check the vertical integration for differences in terms of their ICT environment on the firm-years level. Therefore, I use a cluster analysis to form three groups of country-years that are comparable in terms of their penetration with ICT.[33] I find significant differences in vertical integration of manufacturing firms between these three groups.

Since these differences might be related to a number of other factors than ICT I use a multivariate analysis as a second step to control for alternative explanations. For the multivariate analysis, I aggregate the firm years to the country level and conduct a panel regression. This allows a more detailed study of ICT. I provide evidence for decreasing vertical integration levels in countries with highly developed ICT environments. The analysis is controlled for alternative determinants of firm boundaries at the country level, e.g. the institutional and political environment, market size, as well as research and development (R&D) intensity. I find that highly developed political regimes tend to have less vertically integrated firms which is compatible with the explanation that vertical contracting is easier in politically stable environments

Chapter four presents the research design and the results for the media sector. This part takes a closer look at the global media industry in order to illustrate another form of change in firm boundaries. In particular, I analyze the structural changes in the global media industry focussing on intellectual property rights (IPR) issues. The trend towards increasing vertical

---

[33] This means that e.g. Finland in 1995 might be in the same group with Portugal in 1997 because of similar ICT penetration figures.

integration -that represents a contrast compared to the slimming manufacturing sector- is analyzed and evaluated in terms of efficiency using an eclectic theoretical approach. The theoretical approaches applied comprise TCE, Industrial Organization (IO) Theory, Incomplete Contract Theory, and Public Good Theory. IPR protection is identified as a crucial variable that moderates the impact of ICT on media firm boundaries. The role of IPRs in this context is subsequently checked in a panel regression of recorded music sales. I analyze the impact of ICT penetration in 29 countries over 7 years on per capita sales figures of recorded music. I find that ceteris paribus music sales are significantly lower in environments with high penetration of ICT. In addition, the effects of IPR protection are taken into account regarding their influence on the ICT-IPR relationship. In particular, I analyze in how far the protection of IPRs is enhanced by joining the WIPO Performances and Phonograms Treaty (WPPT). Countries that signed the WPPT do not show the negative relationship between recorded music sales and ICT penetration that exists in environments without WPPT-based IPR protection.

I also study simple and double interaction effects between IPR infringement, WPPT-membership, and the political regime. I find that PC-based copyright infringements occur predominantly in countries with a low-quality political system while peer-to-peer-based infringements take place mainly in more developed political regimes. WPPT-member countries do not show differences in IPR infringement regardless of the quality of their political regime. The analysis indicates that WPPT-membership is decisive for the formation of a transaction environment that saves IPRs from being pirated while the political regime influences the dominant type of piracy. Based on the combination of empirical results and theory synopsis, a conclusion regarding the interaction of media firm boundaries, ICT, and IPR protection is drawn: vertical expansion of media firms is compatible with the interpretation that media firms use hierarchies to protect their IPRs that otherwise are threatened by ICT-enabled copyright infringement.

Chapter five contains the final conclusion that combines the results from the earlier chapters. Based on my theoretical and empirical results I intend to draw a more comprehensive picture of ICT impact on firm boundaries. This allows to gain a more detailed understanding of the central research question at hand: what is the effect of ICT of firm boundaries? Using TCE arguments based on WILLIAMSON (1985, 1991) I find that ICT contributes to the shrinking of firm boundaries in the manufacturing sector but also to their expansion in the media sector. The difference in the impact of ICT can be explained by different aggregate changes in transaction costs. In the manufacturing sector, transaction costs decline on aggregate primarily because of reduced ex-ante transaction costs (e.g. search costs for a transaction partner). For transactions in the media sector, aggregate transaction cost increase because of rising ex-post transaction costs that are the result of ICT-related difficulties in IPR enforcement. The proceeding just described in detail is summarized in the following figure.

Figure 1: Overview

1. Introduction: Includes casual empiricism to motivate the research question, main results, and a detailed description of the proceeding		
1.1 Research Idea and Motivation	1.2 Proceeding + Results	

2. Literature Review: Relates research question to relevant stream of literature and presents existing theoretical and empirical literature on the research question.	
2.1 Firm Boundaries	2.2 Paradigm Choice
2.3 Paradigm Limits and Extensions	2.4 ICT & Firm Boundaries + Portrait of Theoretical Framework: WILLIAMSON '91

3. Manufacturing Sector Analysis: Tests theoretically derived hypotheses of a move-to-the market in manufacturing industry				
3.1 Micro-focus	3.2 Application of Theoretical Framework: WILLIAMSON '91	3.3 Opera-tionalization	3.4 + 3.5 Empirical Tests	3.6 Intermediate Findings

4. Media Sector Analysis: Shows theoretical arguments for ICT-induced media firm boundaries increase, identifies IPRs as crucial factor, test IPR protection empirically				
4.1 Peculiarities of Media Products	4.2 Industry Overview	4.3 Eclectic Theory Survey	4.4 Empirical Analysis	4.5 Intermediate Findings

5. Final Conclusion: Combines results of chapter 3+4 and gives an outlook		
5.1 Comparison of Main Results	5.2 A TCE Motivation for Observed Changes in Firm Boundaries	5.3 Outlook

Source: own figure.

*"I am a dwarf,
but I am standing on
the shoulders of the
giants of the past."*
GIORDANO BRUNO[34]

2. Literature Review

In the following paragraphs, it is shown that the firm boundary changes we recently observed can be motivated within a theoretical context. Therefore, I summarize theoretical and empirical contributions that analyze the determinants of firm boundaries in general and ICT impact on firm boundaries in particular. The theoretical focus is the TCE paradigm that sees the firm as an alternative to the market mechanism to govern a transaction. This paradigm is portrayed in detail (chapter two) and used later in the analysis to rationalize firm boundary changes in the manufacturing (chapter three) and media sector (chapter four). It shows the environmental determinants of firm boundaries

2.1 Determinants of Firm Boundaries: Theory and Evidence

Before summarizing the theory and evidence looking at ICT impact on firm boundaries as a historical progression we have to understand the general determinants of firm boundaries and firm size. KUMAR ET AL (2001) analyze firm boundaries form an international perspective and provide a classification of these theories into *technological* (focus: production function), *institutional* (focus: environmental influences), and *organizational* (focus: process of control) theories.

Having a neoclassical tradition *technological theories* argue that firm boundaries are drawn where the size of the market limits further specialization. Firms will perform tasks subject to increasing returns of scale until the overall size of the industry permits a new firm to specialize in these tasks.[35] Hence, a positive relationship between market size and firm boundaries is expected. The view that firm boundaries reflect the limit of specialization is challenged by BECKER/MURPHY (1992). They argue that division of labor is not solely determined by the size of the market. Increasing market size leads to rising productivity because of specialization effects but productivity is also influenced by other factors. These

---

[34] Cited from ZINGALES (2000), p. 1624.
[35] See STIGLER (1951).

other factors include the coordination of workers that perform complementary specialized jobs and the general amount of knowledge. Hence, the focus of the technological theories is too narrow and other determinants of firm boundaries have to be taken into account.

The *institutional theories* focus on the environmental determinants of firm boundaries. The institutional environment is the "set of fundamental political, social and legal ground rules that establishes the basis for production, exchange and distribution. Rules governing elections, property rights, and the right of contract are examples.[36] Another definition of institutional environment is the totality of political institutions (including the national structure of policymaking, regulation and adjudication) and economic institutions (such as the structure of the national factor markets, the terms of access to international factors of production, and socio-cultural institutions such as informal norms).[37]

KUMAR ET AL (2001) examine the institutional determinants of variation in firm size. The firm size discussion is related but not congruent to the field of vertical integration studies. Nevertheless, the firm size literature is useful to study in order to understand the interaction between firm boundaries and institutional environment. KUMAR ET AL (2001) argue that countries with a better institutional development have bigger firms because firms need external funds to grow.[38] Theses funds are in short supply in environments without properly developed financial markets that are supposed to be more developed in countries with better legal systems.[39] Therefore firm size should be positively correlated with factors that promote the development of financial markets.[40]

BAUR (1990) argues that in systems with weak property protection hierarchical coordination has a comparative advantage over market-based transaction governance. This can be motivated if the financial sphere of the economy is taken into account. More developed

---

[36] DAVIS/NORTH (1971), p. 6-7.

[37] See HENISZ/DELIOS (2002).

[38] There is an important interaction effect in their findings. On average, firms from physical asset intensive industries are smaller compared to firms that are not physical asset intensive (like law and consulting firms) in countries with better judicial systems. The reason for this phenomenon given in this study is that a refined judicial system is necessary to enforce property rights in the latter group of firms (e.g. intellectual property rights) while a crude legal system is sufficient to protect property rights to physical assets, see KUMAR ET AL (2001), p. 2. The peculiarities of protection intellectual property rights are analyzed in detail in chapter four.

[39] See LA PORTA ET AL (1997b).

financial markets that provide external financing facilities are expected to reduce the requirement to build internal capital markets.[41] Following this line of reasoning, we would expect to find smaller but more integrated firms in countries with unsound legal systems. RAJAN/ZINGALES (1998b) found that financial market development positively affects both, firm growth and growth in the total number of firms. Since new firms are usually smaller than existing firms, average firm size decreases with financial market development.

Another fruitful way to look at the relationship between the institutional environment and firm size is to focus on the direct links like contract law etc. Apart from indirect effects of financial markets on firm boundaries there is a connection between the quality of a legal system and firm size as argued by KUMAR ET AL (2001). Studies that concentrate on the direct link between institutional environment and firm boundaries indicate a negative relationship. SCHIFFER/WEDER (2001) found out that the quality of governmental institutions is crucial for small firms. Hence, small legal entities benefit from a sound institutional environment which would again suggest a negative relationship between firm boundaries and institutional environment.

The third group of theories, *organizational theories,* are explaining firm boundaries in the tradition of COASE (1937), and WILLIAMSON (1975, 1985). Within the field of organizational theories, TCE is the principal paradigm for our understanding of firm boundaries, especially vertical integration. The reason is that vertical integration is the main subject of analysis for this theory.[42] TCE research featuring business organization in general and ICT impact on firm boundaries in particular represents the main paradigm of this study.[43] TCE suggests that subsequent stages of the supply chain can be coordinated better via the market mechanism when transaction costs are low. Sound institutional environments provide safer environments

---

[40] See KUMAR ET AL (2001), p. 5. In the same logic, LA PORTA ET AL (1997a) find that firms are larger in high trust societies. Research looking at the interactions of financial and economic development of a country dates back to SCHUMPETER (1942) and GERSCHENKRON (1962).

[41] CLAESSENS ET AL (1999) found that internal markets are more valuable for firms in countries with less-developed financial markets.

[42] In a survey SHELANSKI/KLEIN (1995) found that roughly ¾ of empirical TCE literature (out of 118 journal articles) between 1976 and 1994 are related to vertical integration.

[43] Within this literature (TCE paradigm) there is the most important body of research that looks at the impact of ICT on firm boundaries.

to use this market-based governance forms, e.g. because contracts can be enforced better.[44] Following this line of reasoning I expect a negative relationship between vertical integration and the quality of the institutional environment. In the following paragraphs, I will give a short summary of the central theoretical and empirical contributions to TCE.

The concept of TCE is based on two crucial behavioral assumptions. These assumptions go beyond standard neoclassical reasoning.[45] The first assumption is the bounded rationality of human behavior. The term bounded rationality was coined by SIMON (1957) to describe a lack of information processing competence. Information processing includes the receiving, storing, retrieving, and transmitting of information. Apart from insufficient information, SIMON (1978) considers attention to be the scarce resource in the decision making process. Economic agents intend to act rationally but are restricted by their cognitive capacity. The second is the assumption that human agents are given to opportunism. Opportunism is an extension of neoclassical utility maximization for "self-interest seeking with guile."[46] WILLIAMSON (1985) describes the phenomenon as an "incomplete or distorted disclosure of information, especially the calculated effort to mislead, distort, disguise, obfuscate, otherwise confuse."

COASE (1937) laid the foundation of TCE by introducing the concept of transaction costs into modern economics. He does not mention the term transaction cost explicitly but describes what is usually referred to as transaction costs in the TCE literature.[47] By asking why there are firms in reality and not only markets for coordinating the exchange of goods and services, he provided a motivation for the existence of firms. The 'raison d'être' of a firm is the fact that there are "costs of using the price mechanism". These costs include price discovering costs and costs of negotiating and concluding a separate contract for each exchange transaction. Following COASE (1937), the boundaries of a firm are determined by comparing - at a given technology - the costs of organizing an extra transaction within the firm with the costs of carrying out the same transaction by means of an exchange on the market.

---

[44] WILLIAMSON (1991) argues that market mechanism has advantages in transaction governance compared to hierarchical solutions when the institutional environment (defined as the set of fundamental political, social and legal ground rules) is well established.
[45] WILLIAMSON (1981a).
[46] WILLIAMSON (1985, p.47).
[47] COASE uses terms like "cost of using the price mechanism" or "marketing costs", see COASE (1960, p. 390).

WILLIAMSON (1975, 1985) further developed the TCE paradigm by introducing the topology of markets and hierarchies. Following WILLIAMSON, every transaction has three characteristic features: uncertainty, the frequency with which a transaction occurs, and the degree to which transaction-specific investments are involved (asset specificity). In contrast to frequency and uncertainty, asset specificity is a major transaction dimension.[48] A suitable definition of asset specificity is given in WILLIAMSON (1985, p.55). He defines asset specificity as "durable investments that are undertaken in support of particular transaction, the opportunity cost of which investments is much lower in best alternative uses, or by alternative users, should the original transaction be prematurely terminated."[49] To describe the impact of asset specificity on transactions WILLIAMSON (1985) uses the term "fundamental transformation".

According to WILLIAMSON there are four main types of specificity:[50]

i.   *Site specificity*: in order to minimize certain transaction costs transaction partners are close to each other, e.g. a coal mine and a coal-burning electricity-generating plant are located next to each other to reduce transportation and inventory costs.

ii.   *Physical asset specificity*: one or both transaction parties invest in equipment or machinery that has less value when it is applied in alternative ways.

iii. *Human capital investment*: during a process of social interaction transaction partners acquire relation-specific skills.

iv.   *Dedicated assets*: these comprise general investments made for a specific transaction, e.g. plant extensions to fulfill an extraordinarily huge order.

The profit differential of planned and alternative use of a specific investment is also described as a 'quasi rent'.[51] The phenomenon that one partner captures or appropriates the quasi-rent has been referred to as a 'hold-up'.[52] The distribution of the quasi-rent depends upon the respective negotiating power. Vertical integration can resolve this problem by aligning incentives and thereby suppressing the hold-up incentives.

---

[48] One way to measure the degree of specificity that is given in WILLIAMSON (1981b). He uses opportunity costs, i.e. the costs associated with changing the transaction partner.
[49] Durability of the investment is not necessary to make it specific.
[50] See WILLIAMSON (1985), p. 95.
[51] Comparable concepts in the literature are "composite quasi-rents" by MARSHALL (1952) or "expropriable quasi-rents" by KLEIN ET AL (1978).
[52] ALCHIAN/WOODWARD (1988) analyzed the nature of the asset specificity. They introduced the dimension of plasticity to the discussion. Plastic specific assets are not exposed to hold-ups because the asset vanishes when the owner wants it to (e.g. specialized human capital).

KLEIN ET AL (1978) use a real world example to show the effects of post-contractual opportunistic behavior. They analyze the merger between GM and car body manufacturer Fisher Body (FB). Around 1920 the dominant material to manufacture car bodies changed from wood to steel. In 1919 Fisher Body signed a long-term contract with GM to supply steel car body parts on a cost plus basis. Before 1919 Fisher Body supplied several car manufacturers with wooden car bodies. Under the new contract FM sold almost all its bodies to GM. The new production process required high and idiosyncratic investments in special production technology (a special die). Due to the high specificity of this production technique the FB-GM relationship became a bilateral monopoly. GM could opportunistically renegotiate a lower price because it was the only customer. Similarly, FB (the only producer of the car bodies for GM) could capture the quasi rent by threatening GM with production delay. In the following years, the contract led to huge profits at FB reaping all economies of scale and experiencing strong sales growth. In addition, GM wanted FB to locate close to the GM plants in order to improve the coordination of the production process. This location decision would have made FB even more dependent upon GM. As negotiations with FB became too complex, GM eventually merged with FB to terminate the problematic solution. The market-based business relationship was replaced by a hierarchy through vertical integration.[53]

Following theoretical contributions to TCE a negative relationship of asset specificity and market governance is expected. The theoretical explanations of firm boundaries summarized so far have partially been tested empirically. There is a substantive body of empirical literature that seems to support the theoretical predictions, as noted by MONTEVERDE/TEECE (1982), MASTEN (1984), JOSKOW (1985).

A study by MONTEVERDE/TEECE (1982) is considered to be the first empirical analysis of vertical integration determinants based on TCE arguments. They showed empirically that higher asset specificity in the form of human capital specificity, proxied by the extent of engineering effort in the design process of the respective component, increased the likelihood of vertical integration compared to market procurement. Therefore, the authors examined a sample of 133 components used by GM and Ford in 1976 regarding market-based versus internal procurement.

---

[53] CASADESUS-MASANELL/SPULBER (2000) doubt the asset specificity story. They argue that GM's main objective has been to gain access to the executive talents of FB.

By analyzing the procurement decision of a large aerospace company regarding 1887 components, MASTEN (1984) found further evidence that the likelihood of vertical integration is increased by asset specificity. He demonstrates that the degree of component complexity and design specificity, i.e. the degree of component customization, are significant and positively associated determinants of vertical integration. A test of site specificity, i.e. collocation decisions by firms and its suppliers, yielded no significant results. In a similar study, JOSKOW (1985) analyzes vertical integration between electric utilities and their input providers, i.e. coal mines. He discovered that specific investments operationalized as collocation decision of the mining and electricity generating operations increase the likelihood of vertical integration.

Another important driver of vertical integration is bargaining in 'small number situations' according to WILLIAMSON (1975, 1985). ANDERSON/WEITZ (1986) also consider hierarchies the optimal governance mode in small number situations. They develop a framework for vertical integration decisions in particular in the downstream (sales channel) segment based on TCE. The authors look at the role of vertical integration within the performance determinants of downstream operations. ANDERSON/WEITZ (1986) consider vertical integration to be a moderating variable in the relationship between performance determinants and performance. This view differs from most TCE analyses. However, they make the important observation that TCE has an implicit "bias towards the market mode."[54] The authors argue that hierarchies in TCE frameworks are only desirable in situations with dysfunctional market outcomes.

CAVES/BRADBURD (1988) and MACDONALD (1985) provide evidence that support the theoretical predictions by TCE. CAVES/BRADBURD (1988) found empirically that small-numbers bargaining, lock-in effects, and the necessity to commonly own intangible assets are drivers of vertical integration. A sample of 83 industries supplying intermediate goods is taken. The authors test a vertical integration measure based on the proportion of companies operating in customer and supplier industries. Small-number situations are operationalized by taking a variable that is a combination of several concentration indices. Assets per employee that are specific to the industry and the importance of its output in its customers' cost are used to proxy lock-in effects. R&D sales ratios indicate the necessity to share intangible assets. All

---

[54] ANDERSON/WEITZ (1986), p. 17.

three regressors are significant determinants of vertical integration and thereby support the hypothesis that TCE variables are important determinants of vertical integration.

MACDONALD (1985) looks at the exchange method in the US-American manufacturing sector. He found that vertical integration is preferred to market-based exchange forms in capital intensive industries. The author uses two measures of the degree of vertical integration, total vertical integration (TVI) and manufacturing vertical integration (MVI). TVI is representing the "share of all industry shipments (across all channels) that are directed to establishments owned by the seller."[55] MVI is defined as the "share of industry shipments to manufacturing establishments that are directed internally, to the seller's establishments"[56], i.e. only shipments to manufacturing buyers are included. Since integration between producer-good firms and manufacturers on the one side and manufacturers and retailers on the other side are considered to be different in their integration calculus by the authors the second measure (MVI) is used in the regression analysis. The two measures are highly correlated with a correlation coefficient of 0.94 and show considerable variance. The values for TVI and MVI are in a similar ranges (TVI ranges from 9 to 64, MVI from 8 to 67). Explanatory variables are the seller industry capital intensity (ratio of fixed assets to shipments), seller industry research and development intensity (R&D expenditure to sales), complemented by three measures of market structure. The main result of the study is that buyer and seller concentration both have positive relationships with the vertical integration measure. The same is true for capital intensity while, R&D intensity is not significant.

LIEBERMAN (1991) tested several models of vertical integration based on transaction costs arguments using a data sample from the chemical industry. The author examines several hypotheses that he derives from TCE arguments: (i) small-number situations ex-ante trigger vertical integration, (ii) highly transaction specific investments measured by sunk cost lead to ex-post haggling problems over quasi-rents and thereby make vertical integration more likely, and (iii) the likelihood of vertical integration increases with input cost as a fraction of total production cost for a particular firm.[57] The first hypothesis that backward integration is more likely when a firm faces few upstream suppliers is rejected by the data while hypotheses (ii)

---

[55] MACDONALD (1985), p. 328.
[56] MACDONALD (1985), p. 329.
[57] Hypothesis (iii) states that vertical integration becomes more likely the more important a particular upstream supplier is, i.e. the higher the percentage of delivered inputs from this suppliers is for a particular firm.

and (iii) are supported. Additionally, LIEBERMAN (1991) analyzed the impact of demand variability. Firms that face high demand variability in the input market (upstream) that is uncorrelated with downstream demand variability are prone to integrate backward. In sum, LIEBERMAN (1991) found that integration helps to avoid bargaining problems arising from ex post lock-in.

The studies summarized so far seem to support that TCE can explain variation in vertical integration. However, there are some limitations of the TCE paradigm.

2.2   Paradigm Choice: A Critical Review of Transaction Cost Economics

In order to understand changes in industrial organization with a focus on vertical integration TCE seems to be an apparent paradigm choice. The obvious reason is that the principal question treated by TCE is the understanding of vertical integration. WILLIAMSON called vertical integration the paradigm problem of TCE.[58]

Nevertheless TCE as a theory has been criticized in the literature for the following reasons. An often cited drawback is the low degree of formalization that can be made using the theory.[59] This can be seen as both, its strength and its weakness. On the one hand, it makes the operationalization of theoretically derived hypotheses quite difficult. On the other hand, it increased the set of phenomena (e.g. impact of ICT on firms) that can be analyzed within this approach.[60] It reduces the predictive power of the approach but offers a quasi-universal applicability and therefore explanations for recent organizational changes. Here, a quantified TCE approach is developed to address this general weakness.

TCE also faces inconsistency problems with regard to the bounded rationality assumption. Vertical integration heals the problem of inefficient haggling over quasi-rents provided that these problems are discovered ex ante. Given that the haggling problem is discovered ex post (e.g. due to technological innovation) vertical integration cannot heal the problem because the

---

[58] See WILLIAMSON's introductory overview of TCE in SCHMALENSEE/WILLIG (1989), p. 150.
[59] See SCHUMANN (1992), p. 453. The lack of formality is seen ambiguously: KLEIN ET AL (1978) note that mathematical economics captures only a fraction of the transaction cost phenomenon.
[60] The universality of the Transaction Cost Approach is manifested in the vast variety of analytical subjects it has been applied to, e.g. financial intermediation by LOEFFLER (1991), human resources by WIEGRAN (1993), innovation by PAY (1989).

specific asset is now "in play" like in the case of non-integration.[61] The reason of this problem is inherent in the comparative-static logic of TCE.

A frequently articulated critique of TCE, in particular in the Organizational Behavior (OB) literature, has been targeted towards the opportunism assumption.[62] GHOSHAL/MORAN (1996) argue that opportunism is a self-fulfilling prophecy. They argue that hierarchies are not suitable to cope with opportunistic behavior because all hierarchy-based incentive-alignment mechanisms lead to new opportunism instead of solving the problem. Trust is alleged to be undermined and cooperation discouraged. This reputedly leads to a feedback-loop and opportunistic behavior persists within hierarchies.

A related stream of literature examines if suitable management imperatives can be derived from TCE-based reasoning. Are the results from TCE valuable guidelines for management decisions? GHOSHAL/MORAN (1996) consider TCE to be "bad for practice" and doubt that markets are substitutes for hierarchies because both, markets and hierarchies are too different and have their own distinct and unique logic.

To my mind, the arguments from OB are flawed to some extent. The criticism here stems largely from different scientific roots and traditions (psychological and sociological approaches used by OB scholars and the economics paradigm used in TCE).[63] However, this stream of criticism points at an important object of analysis in economic relations: trust.[64] They argue that the conduct of individuals is not described by the behavioral assumption of opportunism as in TCE but that individuals use trust as an intrinsic motivation. A response from a TCE point of view is that trust can also be integrated into TCE analysis: trust can maintain market-based transaction governance in situations where high asset specificity would suggest integration.[65] The role of trust is an important facet of the problem tackled by

---

[61] See HARM (1996), p. 2.

[62] It is sometimes overlooked that WILLIAMSON assumed only opportunistic behavior in the majority of cases. He stressed the fact that the lack of certainty to correctly assess ex-ante the degree of your transaction partner's opportunistic attitude is a sufficient assumption.

[63] See as a good overview for this school of criticism: GHOSHAL/MORAN (1996).

[64] See e.g. BRADLACH/ECCLES (1989).

[65] Trust can also be modeled within the economic paradigm as a situation in which short-term cheating (opportunistic behavior) is worth less than the discounted value of future co-operation benefits. Approaches from game theory are useful to model this situation formally, see e.g. BINMORE (1992).

TCE that is further deconstructed analytically in the OB literature.[66] Relational governance mechanisms like trust can be used as substitutes for both, contracts and vertical integration.[67]

Despite these alleged weaknesses, TCE has been an influential paradigm to study organizational change and ICT impact on organizational change in particular. Acknowledging transaction costs extended the general-equilibrium modeling in the sense of ARROW/DEBREU (1954) and thereby gave researchers analytical access to a phletora of new economic problems. The approach not to abstract from transaction costs yielded an increase in explanatory power compared to general-equilibrium theory: the existence of firms can be explained. Firms are the result of the existence of transaction costs.

In the following, I will describe some central additions brought to general-equilibrium theory through TCE.

The first important addition is that TCE introduced a concept of the firm as the unit of analysis. The picture of the firm as a production function according to the neoclassical paradigm was replaced by the definition of the firm as a consequence of the existence of transaction costs. This is equivalent to the idea of firm boundaries and a distinction between markets and hierarchies.

The second addition of TCE is that changes in firm boundaries can be understood using the markets versus hierarchies paradigm. For example, merger and acquisition activity can be motivated as the redrawing of efficient firm boundary using TCE terminology. According to TCE, reasons for changes in firm boundaries are occurring because of changing transaction dimensions, i.e. different levels of asset specificity, transaction frequency, or uncertainty.[68] WILLIAMSON (1991) extended the transaction dimensions by introducing the transaction environment as a determinant of firm boundaries. The equilibrium proportion of transactions governed by markets is expressed as a function of the institutional environment. This framework allows to include the transaction environment into the governance decision process.

---

[66] See NOOTEBOOM (1996) for a survey of trust in the context of transaction governance.
[67] Authors developing this arguments are e.g. GRANOVETTER (1985), DYER/SINGH (1998), UZZI (1997).

As shown in the following paragraph information and communication environment represents an important component of the transaction environment and therefore an important determinant of firm boundaries. WILLIAMSON (1991, p. 287) treats the institutional environment as a "set of parameters" that can induce "shifts in the comparative costs of governance"[69]. Applying the WILLIAMSON (1991) framework faces some operationalization problems. These can be mitigated by creating sufficient cross-sectional variance in the institutional setting which is usually achieved in cross-country studies. This makes the "parameter shift" framework a potentially useful tool in cross-country studies of the transaction environment. Chapter 2.5 contains a detailed description of the WILLIAMSON (1991) framework. Before analyzing the impact of the ICT-induced parameter shift in chapter 2.5, I critically review the limits of the TCE framework (chapter 2.3) and summarize the most important contributions analyzing the impact of ICT on firm boundaries (chapter 2.4).

2.3   Limits of the Theory and Paradigm Extensions

HOLMSTRØM/ROBERTS (1998) argue that TCE is still a valuable theory to understand changing firm boundaries but can be criticized for being too focused on the hold-up problem and on the role of asset specificity. They note that investment incentives can be provided by a vast variety of mechanisms of which ownership boundaries represents only one special way. These new incentive mechanisms are fruitful expansions of the original TCE framework.

This view is supported by RAJAN/ZINGALES (2000). They argue that traditional drivers of vertical integration became less important in recent years because of increased competition, especially in markets for intermediate[70] goods. For example, improvements in the financial markets made it easier to raise funds and hence reduced the importance of capital intensity as a protection against competition. Authority in form of employer-employee relationships faces declining importance and is limited by the ability of employees to quit and take their human capital with them.[71] The changes can be grouped into three principal changes in the international business environment that affect firm boundaries:[72]

---

[68] WILLIAMSON (1996, p. 5) argues that TCE traditionally takes the institutional environment as given.
[69] WILLIAMSON (1991, p. 287).
[70] An alternative term for this category of goods is "semi-finished" goods.
[71] See Saatchie and Saatchi example delivered by ZINGALES (2000).
[72] See ZINGALES (2000), p. 1642.

- decreasing specificity of physical assets
- rising importance of human capital as the crucial determinant of firm boundaries
- increasing competition at the intermediate goods level that decreases hold-up risks

Given that traditional determinants of firm boundaries face a declining importance the question is raised if the market versus hierarchy paradigm is still valid. I argue that it is still valid but needs some refinements and expansions.

ZINGALES (2000) described some central refinements of this paradigm. He considers human capital to be the crucial asset, i.e. the explanatory variable for asset specificity and the drawing of firm boundaries. The importance of the topic becomes clear if we look at the effects of the described changes. The revision of TCE has implications for other fields of research. ZINGALES (2000) argues that corporate finance rests upon the concept of the firm developed by TCE. For example, the impact of financing choices can be analyzed only for a known, clear-cut subject of analysis, the firm. In the moment the nature of the firm changes (e.g. its boundaries change and/or become fuzzy), financing decisions are contingent on the new morphology of the firm and the associated interdependencies. ZINGALES (2000) therefore concludes that new insights from TCE affect corporate finance (financing, governance, and valuation).

RAJAN/ZINGALES (2001) argue that the determinant of firm boundaries is the web of specific investments built around a critical resource. The firm is merely a vehicle that provides the employee with the possibility to make specific investments in his own human capital, i.e. to specialize. This leads to a complementary situation between the employee and the firm. Hence, control (not: ownership) over the employee's human capital is exercised by the firm.[73] The acknowledgement of human capital as the key determinant of firm boundaries points at an important organizational change that is going on.

The TCE paradigm extensions mentioned so far are valuable and show that the firm boundaries view is open to extensions. New determinants of firm boundaries, including

---

[73] There are other theories providing alternative determinants of firm boundaries. For example, BADARACCO (1991) argues that reinforced financial and hierarchical control defines the social boundaries of the firm.

human capital and ICT can be integrated into the analysis using the mechanics and arguments from existing TCE research.

A frequent allegation is that the market versus hierarchy paradigm is a continuum that hosts a vast variety of organizational forms. The two extremes (markets and hierarchies) are amended by hybrid forms in the middle.[74] This is equivalent to the argument that we can observe a decreasing degree of dichotomy in organizational forms: the boundaries of the firm are supposed to become blurred, i.e. less distinct.[75] In a dichotomous view, changes in firm boundaries are understood as a shift towards markets or towards hierarchies. Since firm boundaries become more and more blurred changes in firm boundaries are less clear cut. This is the case when a change does not divide a business entity into several new and separate business entities or merge them into one entity but generates an intermediate governance form. These intermediary forms between markets and hierarchies are often classified as hybrids.[76] Organizational forms subsumed under this term include e.g. joint ventures, alliances, and long-term supplier relationships. The notion that there is a distinct organization form called "hybrid" between the two extremes is acknowledged by WILLIAMSON (1991).[77] He considers hybrids to be optimal transaction governance mechanisms in situations with intermediate asset specificity.

There are several approaches to treat hybrids within the TCE paradigm. One extension of the markets versus hierarchy paradigm that uses a distinct hybrid form is the introduction of clans by OUCHI (1980) and OUCHI/WILLIAMSON (1981). Here, hierarchies are reinterpreted as bureaucracies and clans are added as a third governance vehicle. This third form of governing a transaction stands for the impact of common socialization pattern like values and norms on the behavior of individuals. Transactions executed by members of an organization are not necessarily driven and controlled by authority and 'fiat' but by the employees' natural inclination.

---

[74] See e.g. RICHARDSON (1972) for an early form of this argument.
[75] See RAJAN/ZINGALES (2000).
[76] A related term for this group of organizational forms is „relational forms" of organizations, see DAY/WENDLER (1998), p. 12. MENARD (1996) argues that different types of hybrids can simultaneously govern a transaction. For a discussion on the necessity to develop a topology of hybrid forms of governance see MENARD (2002). A topology of the most important hybrid governance forms is given in RIEMER ET AL (2001).
[77] WILLIAMSON (1991) extended his own paradigm by introducing the notion of a hybrid as a third distinct governance form between markets and hierarchies.

Another extension of TCE that accounts for the existence of hybrids is the AGIL scheme which was originally developed by PARSONS/SMELSER (1956) and extended by KLEIN (1996). It can be interpreted as an extension of the TCE framework but also allows to analyze the impact of ICT on business organization. The unit of analysis used by the AGIL scheme are systems of interaction between collective and individual actors, i.e. social systems. The scheme differentiates between four basic functions of these systems that guarantee their functionality and adaptability. The four basic functions are summarized in the following figure:

Figure 2: AGIL Scheme

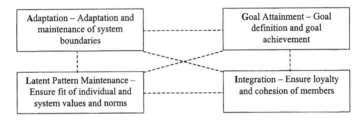

Source: translated from KLEIN (1996), p. 94.

KLEIN (1996) used the AGIL scheme to extend the market versus hierarchies paradigm. Besides markets and hierarchies, he adds two additional governance mechanisms, i.e. networks and negotiation systems. Since each governance mechanism uses another means of coordination, KLEIN allocates a corresponding dimension of the AGIL scheme to all four governance mechanisms. The modified AGIL scheme is presented in the following figure:

Figure 3: Modified AGIL Scheme following KLEIN (1996)

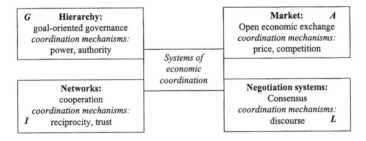

Source: translated from KLEIN (1996), p. 98.

A market is a governance structure that is characterized by decentral coordination and spontaneous order.[78] In the AGIL scheme, markets correspond to the adaptation dimension (A-dimension). Hierarchies, e.g. firms, use power and authority as principal means of coordination. Since transaction governance is achieved 'by fiat' hierarchies are considered to be goal-oriented governance mechanisms in the AGIL scheme, i.e. correspond to the G-dimension.

In addition, KLEIN (1996) introduces networks and negotiation systems as alternative governance mechanisms. Networks are cooperative coordination forms between autonomous but interdependent firms that correspond to the integration dimension (I-Dimension) of the AGIL scheme. The L-Dimension of the AGIL scheme, latent pattern maintenance, is achieved via negotiation systems. Here, coordination is achieved via a discourse that leads to a consensus.[79]

The AGIL scheme delivers a viable interpretation of the intermediate zone between markets and hierarchies. Thereby it represents a bridge between TCE and network research that focuses on the role of interorganizational information systems (IOS).[80] In order to make the AGIL scheme susceptible for empirical analysis, an appropriate operationalization of the intermediate governance forms like networks is indispensable. The appropriateness of financial statement data – that will form the backbone of my analysis – as a basis to operationalize the AGIL scheme is debatable. Contract analysis[81] or questionnaire-based research might be more beneficial in this context. Hence, for data availability reasons I use a 'pure' TCE research design based on the WILLIAMSON (1991) framework which suits best the purpose of this analysis. Nevertheless, the AGIL scheme should be seen as a successful example of how to extend the TCE paradigm.

---

[78] See KLEIN (1996) quoting HAYEK (1969), p. 32-46.

[79] KLEIN further refines each AGIL dimension and develops a topology of networks which is omitted here. However, the general description of the AGIL scheme is sufficient to understand the AGIL scheme as an extension of WILLIAMSON's TCE paradigm.

[80] See KLEIN (1996), p. 39-60.

[81] According to COASE (2002), a way to study the impact of ICT on firm boundaries and thereby extend the TCE paradigm is contract analysis. This could be a task for future research treating the same subject (ICT impact on firm boundaries in an international comparison) with a different tool-set as soon as the contract data will be available. A major project to study economic activity empirically using the contract paradigm is the Contracting and Organizational Research Institute (CORI) at the University of Missouri in Columbia. In contrast to the

In a nutshell, TCE seems to be a defendable and intuitive paradigm choice to systemize the mechanisms that determines firm boundaries in general, and vertical integration in particular. As shown in the following paragraph it also allows to include new determinants of firm boundaries. An important but rather new determinant of firm boundaries is ICT. COASE (2002), who can be seen as the inventor of TCE, notes that ICT has an influence on transaction costs by stating: transaction costs are "affected by technological factors. And one example which is very much discussed today is the influence on transaction costs, and on the organization of industry, of the development of the Internet."[82]

Another important point is that the institutional environment is increasingly characterized by technological factors. For example, OXLEY/YEUNG (2001) study the institutional environment by focussing on cross-country variation in penetration with ICT. Recent studies like OXLEY/YEUNG (2001) show that the importance of ICT as a determinant of a country's institutional environment is still growing.

The next chapter includes a survey of the theoretical and empirical literature looking at the impact of the ICT shock on firm boundaries.

2.4 Impact of Information and Communication Technology on Firm Boundaries
2.4.1 Theory

Research that studies the effect of modern ICT on economic activity and business organization is a young but growing field of the literature.[83] Precursors of research treating the impact of ICT on firm boundaries look at effects of electronic information processing devices on corporate organization and date back to the early 1970s. Then, interorganizational information systems consisted largely of proprietary technology and have been highly specific. Hence, vertical integration was supposed to increase.[84] Thereafter, improving IT structures and increasing standardization of IT devices pointed towards advantages of IT-supported decentralized structures.[85]

---

financial statement data used in my analysis the contract data to conduct empirical analyses with CORI is not yet available.

[82] COASE (2002), p. 6.

[83] Recently, the stream of research looking at ICT impact on firm boundaries has been fuelled by research on Internet-based electronic commerce (E-Commerce), see e.g. GARICANO/KAPLAN (2000) or BAKOS (2001).

[84] KAUFMANN (1966), p. 152, STERN/CRAIG (1971), p. 85.

[85] See BAUER (1997), p.199.

The most important body of literature looking at the ICT impact on firm boundaries uses TCE logic. This line of research started more or less with an influential paper by MALONE ET AL (1987). Their seminal paper suggests an ICT-triggered increase in the efficiency of markets and hierarchies to govern transactions. MALONE ET AL (1987) use a dichotomous organizational view by differentiating between markets and hierarchies. They differentiate between an electronic communication effect, an electronic brokerage effect, and an electronic integration effect.[86] The key determinants of the governance choice are product specificity and the complexity of the product description.[87] The authors argue that the overall effect will be an increase in market governance compared to hierarchical governance mechanisms mainly as a result of decreasing asset specificity.[88] The two central arguments of the 'move-to-the-market hypothesis' by MALONE ET AL (1987) are:

> "[S]ince the essence of coordination involves communicating and processing information, the use of information technology seems likely to decrease these costs [...]."[89]

and

> "[T]he result of reducing coordination costs without changing anything else should be an increase in the proportion of economic activity coordinated by markets."[90]

GURBAXANI/WHANG (1991) analyze the same question by using both transaction cost theory and agency theory type arguments. Their contribution is to refine the TCE calculus that trade-off between production cost (lower in market settings) and transaction cost (lower in hierarchies) determines the most efficient governance mode. TCE neglects to some extent the processes within a hierarchy or firm, i.e. the internal coordination costs. These processes can be described by minimizing the sum of decision information costs[91] (presumably lower when

---

[86] The electronic communication effect is a term that subsumes the effect of faster and less costly use of more information. The electronic integration effect stands for the ICT-enabled combination of different, previously separated functions (e.g. vertical production stages) into a single one, e.g. by avoiding media disruptions. The electronic brokerage effect subsumes all ICT-triggered disintermediation of middlemen.

[87] See MALONE ET AL (1987), p. 486.

[88] Similarly, EBBERS (1994) supports the "move-to-the-market" on a theoretical basis by conjecturing that the optimal degree of asset specificity is changing due to increasing scale and scope of transactions.

[89] MALONE ET AL (1987), p. 486.

[90] MALONE ET AL (1987), p. 491.

[91] Decision information costs include information processing costs and opportunity costs due to poor information, see GURBAXANI/WHANG (1991), p. 62.

decision rights are decentralized) and agency costs[92] (presumably lower when decision rights are centralized). The authors argue that ICT changes the trade-off between decision information cost and monitoring cost. Since ICT is able to improve employee monitoring and reduce information processing cost at the same time, the overall result is unclear. Therefore, the impact on total internal coordination cost is unclear, too.

One merit of GURBAXANI/WHANG (1991) is to emphasize that ICT also has an impact on the cost of using a hierarchy. This additional aspect is obtained by using agency theory in addition to TCE. The extension of TCE arguments with an agency cost calculus is ambivalent. I follow HART (1995) who considers the principal agent view to be inappropriate for organizational studies. The reason is that the principal agent view is consistent with both, one huge firm in the world that consists of numerous divisions linked by optimal incentive contracts and many small firms linked by optimal arm's-length contracts.[93] Therefore, TCE is a more suitable theoretical foundation for the research focus of this study.

The second merit of GURBAXANI/WHANG (1991) is to introduce the idea of value-added partnerships (VAP) that obtain operational economies of scale by being vertically small and horizontally large as an alternative or substitute to vertical integration. This shows that changes in firm boundaries can remain undetected, for example if hybrid governance mechanisms and quasi- or partial vertical integration[94] constructs are used.

However, GURBAXANI/WHANG's (1991) paper broadens the coarse view of MALONE ET AL (1987) by reminding that firm-internal transactions are also affected by information technology variables. The theoretical outcome of the impact of ICT remains a function of the individual constellation of internal and external coordination cost. PICOT ET AL (2001, p. 407) support the view of GURBAXANI/WHANG (1991) by stating that ICT can reduce intra-firm coordination costs to the same extent as inter-firm coordination costs.[95]

---

[92] Agency cost are e.g. the principal's (employer's) cost of monitoring an agent (employee), the bonding cost of the agent and the residual loss, see JENSEN/MECKLING (1976).
[93] HART (1995), p. 20.
[94] Hybrid governance mechanisms include value-added partnerships, firm networks. For a discussion of hybrids as governance form see e.g. MENARD (2002).
[95] See PICOT ET AL (2001), p. 407.

BAKOS (1992) makes an important contribution to this question by arguing that the effect of ICT on *intra*organizational coordination and production cost seem to be more ambivalent than on *inter*organizational coordination.[96] Historically, we can observe that ICT has been primarily used to support internal (hierarchical) coordination, e.g. via the implementation of enterprise resource planning (ERP) software. BROUSSEAU (1999) points out that newer forms (e.g. interorganizational information systems (IOS)[97] like the Internet) are supposed to bring more productivity gains in market-based transactions. The view that new ICTs led to a restructuring of corporate hierarchies in the 1980s and early 1990s while the present ICT applications tend to produce structural changes in inter-company relationships[98] is supported by TAPSCOTT (1995, p. 97). He further notes that the present ICT applications created the beginning of a connected business architecture. This would mean that recent developments in ICT affect organizational design primarily via reducing the cost of *inter*organizational coordination.

The prediction of a 'move-to-the-market' has been questioned in the literature. An interesting modification of the trend towards market governance has been found by CLEMONS/ROW (1992) and CLEMONS ET AL (1993). They found that, on average, investments in IT-based coordination between firms show low specificity and improve the ability of the firm to monitor compliance with arm's-length contracts. Hence, market-based transactions become more advantageous compared to internal transactions. The caveat is that firms seem to move towards more market governance as a result of improved IT, but tend to rely on fewer business partners with whom the buyer has long-term relationships. Quasi-integration in the form of long-term contracts seem to be the most efficient governance structure in terms of incentive-compatibility. This effect ('outsourcing cum fewer business partners') is often referred to as the 'move-to-the-middle hypothesis'. Similar results have been found by CUSUMANO/TAKEISHI (1991).

BAKOS/BRYNJOLFSSON (1997) have a comparable line of arguments. They explain situations with 'outsourcing cum fewer business partners' by emphasizing the need to account for non-

---

[96] BAKOS (1992) emphasizes that ICT decreases *inter*organizational coordination cost by reducing problems from small-number situations, e.g. via the implementation of *inter*ogranisational information systems.

[97] According to KLEIN (1996, p. 40), IOS are information systems combining two or more organizational entities with the objective of an exchange or common use of information or data. KLEIN (1997, p. 51) notes that an important role of IOS is to enable firms to exchange standardized messages with a minimal amount of human intervention.

contractible investments[99] that firms need when conducting business electronically. The limiting force of ICT induced outsourcing can be attributed to reputation and trust effects. Thus, in situations with substantial transaction cost, the efficiency improvement due to integration can also be achieved by integration substitutes, i.e. reputation mechanisms and relationship building.

Like the 'move-to-the-market hypothesis', the 'move-to-the-middle hypothesis' has been challenged. HOLLAND/LOCKETT (1997) go further by arguing that there is no general rule in the relationship between IT and governance mode. The efficient mix of the two types of coordination mechanisms (markets and hierarchies) is determined on a case-to-case basis. The result can e.g. be an implementation of market mechanisms within a hierarchy and vice versa. They argue further that the impact of IT depends upon firm and industry characteristics which means that the same type of IT can do harm in one firm and be beneficial in another firm. According to HOLLAND/LOCKETT (1997) the divergence of this impact increased over time. This has been referred to as the 'mixed modes of operations hypothesis' or 'anything goes hypothesis'.

A second interface to plug in the ICT impact on firm boundaries into a TCE framework is the set of assumptions. A key proposition of TCE is that individuals intend to be rational but their rationality is bounded-constrained by the environment in which they operate and their own human limitations.[100] Lacking all the information needed, the formulation of a set of alternatives to choose from becomes incomplete. The results are personal biases and consequently incomplete contracts.[101] ICT is supposed to decrease the effect of bounded rationality by taking away limits on information processing and communication capacity. WILLIAMSON (1987) argued that without limits on this capacity (i.e. in situations with very low bounded rationality), any type of opportunistic behavior can be anticipated and provided for in perfectly contingent contracts leading to ceteris paribus more market governance.

---

[98] For example in form of interorganizational information systems (IOS).
[99] Examples for non-contractible investments given by BAKOS/BRYNJOLFSSON (1997) are: improving quality, information sharing, and innovation.
[100] See Simon (1978).
[101] Incomplete Contract Theory represents a stream of research that is related to TCE. For seminal contributions, see GROSSMAN/HART (1986), HART/HOLMSTRØM (1987).

A third theoretical line of reasoning explaining the impact of ICT on transaction governance can be modeled as a mechanism that ceteris paribus reduces the probability of 'small-number situations' and the necessity for (relation-)specific investments in vertical relationships. BAKOS/BRYNJOLFSSON (1997, p. 4) argue that ICT in the form of electronic marketplaces suppresses small-number situations that foster opportunistic behavior by providing a large number of potential trading partners. Electronic marketplaces facilitate the finding of an appropriate transaction partner which lowers transaction costs in the form of search costs.[102] Open access to an electronic marketplace guarantees choice of the transaction partner and thereby reduces the necessity for (relationship-)specific investments.[103] The providers of these marketplaces can also offer secure electronic payment systems to further enhance trust between the trading partners.[104] ICT also enables firms to communicate electronically real-time information regarding inventory and demand levels at each stage of production in ICT-supported Just-In-Time (JIT) supply chains.[105] Thus, the importance of vertical integration as an incentive alignment mechanism decreases.

The synopsis of related theoretical contributions demonstrates that the outcome is not unambiguous. There are arguments for and against a 'move-to-the-market'. Hence, the overall result of ICT impact still remains an empirical question. But the survey of theoretical work helps to identify the principal determinants of vertical integration that are needed for an empirical approach to this question which I now will turn to.

2.4.2 Evidence

GARICANO/KAPLAN (2000) studied the impact of ICT on transaction costs and found a negative relationship. Following MILGROM/ROBERTS (1992, p. 29), GARICANO/KAPLAN (2000) differentiate between coordination costs that are mainly caused by opportunism and motivation cost that are mainly caused by bounded rationality. Coordination costs are defined as the cost that result from the need to determine a price and to communicate the

---

[102] BROWN/GOOLSBEE (2000) found that the Internet has the power to significantly reduce consumer search costs by providing consumers with low-cost online price comparisons. This also applies for business sector transactions.

[103] Relationship-specific investments are investments in assets that have a large discrepancy in value in its second best use, compared to its first best use. For the distinction between general purpose assets and relation-specific assets see LEVINTHAL/FICHMAN (1988), and DYER/SINGH (1998).

[104] An overview of the principal electronic payment technologies and a description of a particular payment technology is given e.g. in BENDER (2001).

[105] See BROUSSEAU (1999), p. 4.

characteristics of a transaction including the existence and location of the transaction partners. This includes the costs of obtaining information[106], the costs of coordination inputs,[107] and measurement costs[108]. The costs associated with the incompleteness and the asymmetry of information as well as imperfect commitment are termed motivation costs.[109] The latter cost type includes agency cost[110] and the cost of haggling over quasi-rents.[111]

GARICANO/KAPLAN (2000) look at the impact of ICT in the form of the Internet on transaction costs. This impact can be classified into (a) implications for coordination costs and (b) on motivation costs. The impact on coordination costs can be subdivided into three major subcategories: (i) process improvements in form of interest and depreciation cost for cars to be sold, (ii) marketplace benefits, and (iii) indirect improvements. ICT implications for motivation costs are consequences for (i) information asymmetries in form of adverse selection costs, and for (ii) imperfect commitment. The authors studied transaction data for an Internet-based car marketplace and found that coordination cost are lowered while motivation costs in the form of informational asymmetries remained constant compared to physical transactions.[112] The overall effect is a decrease in transaction costs.

According to TCE theory we would expect shrinking firm boundaries. There is some evidence, at the industry level, that increases in investment in IT were indeed associated with a decline in average firm size and a rise in the number of firms. In an empirical test, BRYNJOLFSSON ET AL (1994) found support for the ICT-triggered 'move-to-the-market hypothesis'. The authors summarize the theoretical literature by stating that IT will reduce internal and external coordination cost. Hence, the impact of IT on firm size remains an empirical question. They could show that firm size decreased with employment of information technology using data for six sectors of the economy. Different measures of firm size are tested including ones based on the number of employees, net sales, and another based on value-added.

---

[106] See STIGLER (1961).
[107] See ALCHIAN/DEMSETZ (1972).
[108] See BARZEL (1982).
[109] See MILGROM/ROBERTS (1992).
[110] See JENSEN/MECKLING (1976).
[111] See WILLIAMSON (1975, 1985), KLEIN ET AL (1978).
[112] The costs of imperfect commitment, i.e. ex-post transaction cost, are not tackled empirically by GARICANO/KAPLAN (2000).

Using industry-level data from 1976 to 1989 on IT capital they found evidence for reductions in firm size caused by increased use of IT. The hypothesis explored by BRYNJOLFSSON ET AL is that increasing use of IT changes the relative viability of small and large firms. The dependent variable shows increasing relative viability of small firms. The two principal theoretical explanations for this conjectured relationship are either labor substitution or changes in the 'make versus buy' strategy of the firm. The labor substitution hypothesis explains the above relationship by firms that substitute employees by IT and produce the same output with fewer people.[113] The 'make versus buy' hypothesis is another form of the 'move-to-the-market hypothesis' and conjectures that outsourcing is easier with increasing availability of IT. If the latter hypothesis was true the data would be supposed to show decreases in all firm size measures (employees, sales, and value-added) while the first hypothesis would be visible in form of decreases in the employee measures but constant or increasing sales and value-added figures.[114]

Firm size is operationalized by BRYNJOLFSSON ET AL (1994) using four different measures: (i) number of employees per establishment[115], (ii) number of employees per firm, (iii) sales per firm, and (iv) value-added per firm. Over a period of five years the authors showed that doubling the IT stock in an industry triggers a decrease of approximately 12% in average value-added per firm. The employee measures also show a negative correlation with the IT variables. The authors argued that the decline in all measures of firm size is consistent with the hypothesis that IT decreases vertical integration. If only the employee measures but not value-added and sales were negatively correlated with the IT variables the labor substitution hypothesis would be a valid alternative explanation. This is not the case. Since all measures show a decline, the 'make versus buy' or outsourcing hypothesis is a more appealing explanation.[116] The results support the 'move-to-the-market hypothesis' by finding that IT – with a one to two year time lag– leads to decreases in the employee measures of firm size while the latter two measures, sales and value-added remained more or less unchanged. A similar result has been found earlier by KAMBIL (1991). In a cross-industry study, KAMBIL

---

[113] There is very few evidence that supports a substitutive relationship between labor and IT in the existing literature. IT and labor seem to be complements, see BERNDT/MORRISON (1991).

[114] BRYNJOLFSSON ET AL (1994), p. 1631.

[115] The term business establishment is, strictly speaking, not an equivalent to the term firm. The authors use data from a database called 'County Business Patterns' Annual Summaries' that uses a slightly different definition of a firm. However, a study by CARLSSON (1988) showed that the correlation between changes in the number of establishments and the number of firms is over 97%, see BRYNJOLFSSON ET AL (1994), p. 1634.

[116] See BRYNJOLFSSON ET AL (1994), p. 1631.

(1991) found that higher buy/make ratios are associated with an increase in investment of the capital stock in information technology IT.[117]

In contrast to earlier industry-level studies, SHIN (2002) and HITT (1998) use firm-level data. Both authors found further support for IT-driven decreases in vertical integration using firm-level data for the US.

SHIN (2002) uses an economy-wide US firm level dataset from 1988 to 1992 to test the relationship between IT and vertical integration. The vertical integration measure defined as the ratio of value-added to total sales is obtained from Compustat data by subtracting the costs of raw materials from the value of production. The value of production is determined by subtracting the beginning inventory from the sum of 'ending inventory' and 'total sales'. Subtracting 'labor and overhead expenses' from 'costs of good sold' delivers the value-added figure.[118] Alternative determinants of vertical integration are taken into account by controlling the analysis for asset specificity (operationlized as R&D expenditure), uncertainty (operationalized as firm beta, i.e. systematic risk), year, and industry specific effects. SHIN (2002) found that IT spending is negatively correlated with vertical integration in a significant way. The uncertainty measure shows an expected and significant positive correlation with vertical integration for the full sample, while R&D expenditure correlates significantly with increasing vertical integration only for the manufacturing sector sub-sample.

HITT (1998) added a horizontal integration measure to the same question. He analyzed the theoretical prediction that IT reduces both, internal and external coordination cost. To examine this relationship he tested the hypothesis that IT leads to increased diversification (horizontal integration) and decreased vertical integration. The author tests a model using a panel data set of information technology capital stock, firm structure, and relevant control variables for 549 large firms from 1987 to 1994. Vertical integration is operationalized using the vertical industry connection index (VIC) by MADDIGAN (1981). This index shows commodity flows (i.e. input-output dependencies) between two industries in which a firm participates working with aggregate input-output tables for the U.S. economy. The IT variable

---

[117] Although the study used only a two-digit SIC code level it received credits to be one of the first empirical papers in this context.
[118] The author states that the costs of raw materials were not available from Computstat.

is based on survey data of IT hardware market value. Diversification is measured with the Herfindahl index[119] and the number of industries (SIC codes) in which the firm operates.

HITT (1998) found that substantial decreases in vertical integration and weak increases in diversification can be attributed to the use of IT. This is also true when the analysis is performed for changes in IT capital and firm structure. The results show a significant negative relationship between vertical integration and IT both, on the firm level and by aggregating the data on the industry level. Interestingly, causality is not one-directional in this context: controlling for alternative determinants of IT demand, HITT points out that firms with low degrees of vertical integration have a high demand for IT. The contribution of HITT's article is to add the dimension of horizontal integration to the analysis and to account for reverse causality. Like many of his predecessors HITT is unable to include forms of quasi-integration (e.g. long term contracts or other hybrid forms of cooperation) in his analysis.

CARLSSON (1988) analyzed the metal-working industry. Using data between 1972 and 1982, he found that vertically integrated firms were 'decoupling', thereby generating smaller firms. According to CARLSSON (1988) this effect can be attributed to the increased usage of IT.

The synopsis so far showed that there is substantial evidence for the impact of ICT at the firm[120] and industry[121] level. One reason for the finding that the impact of ICT on firm boundaries cannot be detected on the country level has to do with the level of analysis. Due to aggregation diverging firm-specific effects of ICT cannot be detected in studies at the country level as in KOHLI/SHERER (2002). The missing effect of ICT can be explained using the 'move-to-the-middle hypothesis' by HOLLAND/LOCKETT (1997): the implications of ICT for the organizational shape are firm-specific.

This also applies to the ICT impact on productivity: A study of the MCKINSEY GLOBAL INSTITUTE (2001) analyzes the contribution of information technology (IT) to the sharp US productivity growth increase from 1995-2000.[122] This study reveals that IT investments are not the main driver of this economy-wide productivity increase. Factors like cyclical demand

---

[119] The Herfindahl index is a common measure of industry concentration, see e.g. TIROLE (1992), p. 482.
[120] E.g. SHIN (2002) and HITT (1998).
[121] E.g. KAMBIL (1991).

and innovation were identified as more important factors. The phenomenon that IT investments seem not to lead to productivity increases is known as the 'productivity paradox'. SOLOW (1987) argued that "[w]e see the computer age everywhere except in the productivity statistics."[123]

But there is also country-level evidence that can serve as an indicator and a cross- or double-check for the hypothesized relationship of a 'move-to-the-market'. KRUGMAN (1995) calls this empirical pattern of macroeconomic data "slicing the value chain". Vertical disintegration and the break-up of value-chains observed from a macro perspective would lead to growing intra-industry trade. The flow of intermediate goods that used to take place within a firm become visible as trade if firms disintegrate vertically. In fact, international transactions show not only increasing trade-shares of GDP for the US and many other OECD countries but also more merchandise trade as a share of merchandise value-added.[124] HUMMELS EL AL (1998) attribute this finding to vertical-specialization-based trade due to specialization of a country in particular segments of the value chain. In fact, empirical studies for many OECD countries using a vast variety of measures show the increased use of imported inputs and a narrowing of production activities within each country.[125]

In addition, KOZICKI (1997) found a widening gap between manufacturing and services productivity growth.[126] Like in the trade data pattern, increased outsourcing has been found to be a reason for the widening. In the KOZICKI study, adjacent stages of a value-chain are no longer coordinated by a single firm (a manufacturing firm with service functions) but take place in different entities (service firm and a manufacturing firm).[127] This is consistent with BRYNJOLFSSON ET AL (1994, p. 1629) who found that the number of employees per firm has declined in manufacturing but not in the service sector.

---

[122] From 1995-2000 US productivity growth grew at an annual rate of 2.5% which is nearly twice the 1972-1995 average. In the same time period the velocity of IT investments doubled.

[123] BRYNJOLFSSON ET AL (2000) identify one reason that can lead to the productivity paradox: the temporal structure of the benefits from IT investments, i.e. that some benefits of ICT accrue in form of organizational capital. By using Tobin's q to measure the intangible assets in the form of organizational capital created through IT investments the authors capture the discounted future value of these benefits that is positive.

[124] FEENSTRA/HANSON (1997), FEENSTRA (1998).

[125] FEENSTRA (1998).

[126] When employment in the manufacturing sector decreases because particular tasks are outsourced to a business services firm, manufacturing employment declines and business services employment increases. This is the case even though the same task is performed.

[127] In Germany, nominal value-added the manufacturing sector slumped from over 40% in 1970 to 28% today while the service sector rose from 42% to 60%, see GROEMLING ET AL (1998).

2.4.3 Literature Summary

The literature review shows that there is empirical work that scrutinizes the determinants of firm boundaries in general and vertical integration in particular. We also have empirical studies and a growing stream of research looking at the impact of ICT that builds on the findings of earlier vertical integration research. In a nutshell, the majority of the evidence in the literature is not contradictory to the view that interorganizational coordination has ceteris paribus been improved by ICT via making market governance easier. Appendix I includes a structured overview of the principal contributions studying the determinants of firm boundaries and the role of ICT in this context.

The question remains why a cross-country view of ICT impact on firm structure is still missing. The reason for the lack of international studies on ICT impact on firm boundaries is partly the limited availability of data. Another related cause is that ICT, especially in its interorganizational form and its international distribution is a relatively new phenomenon. Intertemporal and cross-country variance in the availability of ICT is a rather young phenomenon. The international analysis is thereby not understood as a special case of the analyzed relationship between transaction governance and ICT but simply used as a variance generator for the institutional determinants of the analyzed relationship.

TCE-based research on the impact of ICT on firm boundaries started with MALONE ET AL (1987) and developed a significant body of literature that has been summarized above. KUMAR ET AL (2001) made a first and substantial step towards drawing an international picture of firm boundaries but did not include the ICT stream of research. I study firm boundaries and their relationship with ICT on an international level by combining these two bodies of literature. The following figures graphically summarized the state of research dealing with the impact of ICT on firm boundaries.

Figure 4: Firm Boundaries Research

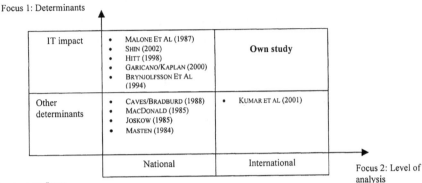

Focus 1: Determinants

			Own study
IT impact	• MALONE ET AL (1987) • SHIN (2002) • HITT (1998) • GARICANO/KAPLAN (2000) • BRYNJOLFSSON ET AL (1994)		**Own study**
Other determinants	• CAVES/BRADBURD (1988) • MACDONALD (1985) • JOSKOW (1985) • MASTEN (1984)	• KUMAR ET AL (2001)	
	National	International	

Focus 2: Level of analysis

Source: own figure.

In order to theoretically derive hypotheses that account for both foci of the existing literature an appropriate theoretical research design is needed. I choose the WILLIAMSON (1991) framework because it allows to analyze variations in the institutional transaction environment including differences in the availability of ICT with an international sample. The international scope of the analysis allows to assess how differences in ICT and other institutional features affect transaction governance. The following chapter gives a brief overview of the WILLIAMSON (1991) framework.

2.5 The Impact of Information and Communication Technology on Firm Boundaries as a Parameter Shift: WILLIAMSON (1991)

From the TCE point of view presented in WILLIAMSON (1991), changes in transaction costs are supposed to influence firm boundaries. To understand the impact of changing transaction costs on organization a clear definition of transaction costs is needed. There is still some confusion and disagreement about the appropriate definition of transaction cost in the literature.[128] An early concept of the term has been developed by COMMONS (1934). He understands a transaction as the "alienation and acquisition between individuals of the rights of future ownership of physical things".[129] This definition focuses on the transfer of sanctioned property rights. Later, ARROW (1969) associated transaction costs in a more

---

[128] See SAALBACH (1996), p. 3-5
[129] COMMONS (1934), p. 64.

general sense with "the costs of running the economic system".[130] The term has been further developed by WILLIAMSON using a broader concept of transaction:

> "*A transaction occurs when a good or service is transferred across a technologically separable interface. One stage of activity terminates and another begins.* "[131]

Thereby the transaction is seen as the atom of microeconomic behavior, i.e. "the ultimate unit of microanalytical analysis".[132] The costs associated with coordinating a transaction are transaction costs. WILLIAMSON (1985) uses the contract paradigm to describe these coordination costs. Transaction costs can be divided up into three main categories[133]: the costs of (i) preparing (searching, negotiating), (ii) concluding, and (iii) enforcing (controlling, adopting) contracts. Preparing contracts includes all search and information costs. (i) and (ii) belong to the category of ex ante transaction costs, (iii) comprises all ex post transaction costs.

NORTH/WALLIS (1994) use a different definition of transaction costs, which I do not adopt in this study. Their definition takes a more macro-orientated view and tries to measure the amount of transaction cost in the economy as a whole. According to NORTH/WALLIS (1994) a good or a service has a set of characteristics. This set consists of physical attributes (size, shape, color, location etc.) on the one side and the property rights to the good on the other side (right to use, right to derive income from etc.). Altering physical attributes evokes transformation or production costs whereas transferring the property rights is associated with transaction costs.

Changes in transaction costs have implications for the optimal governance structure of economic activity. TCE uses the concept of a trade-off between production costs advantages of outside procurement and transaction costs advantages of internal production to explain particular organizational designs for economic activity. The overall sum of production and

---

[130] ARROW (1969), p. 48.
[131] WILLIAMSON (1985), p. 1.
[132] WILLIAMSON (1975), p. xi.
[133] See WILLIAMSON (1985), p. 22 or PICOT (1982).

transaction cost (cost of using the price mechanism)[134] determines the efficient governance structure for a transaction.

The relationship between transaction cost and firm boundaries can be explained using a vertical industry relationship. Supposed that a number of final goods producers downstream want to procure a specialized, indivisible input from an upstream supplier. The two possible governance structures for this procurement transaction are: (i) arm's-length market procurement, or (ii) 'integrated procurement' (after a merger between the two firms).[135] The procurement decision influences vertical structure of the observed group of firms. Due to the sunk cost of producing the input in a specialized way, the downstream buyer knows that under arm's-length governance he might face a hold-up by the supplier and thereby fails to recoup its cost ex-post.[136] The integrated solution is expected to safeguard the up- and downstream firm against hold-ups at the cost of implementing a hierarchical structure, i.e. the costs of a merger and the higher governance cost associated with managing the bigger firm.[137] By integrating vertically the market mechanism is replaced by a coordination structure that combines the locus of decision-making for the respective activity under the management of a single firm. According to JOSKOW (1988), vertical integration "is simply a means of coordinating the different stages of an industry value chain when bilateral trading is not beneficial."[138]

However, there are limitations regarding this view. According to the TCE view, a firm is a set of commonly owned assets which corresponds to the legal definition. Recent contributions to firm boundary research[139] go further and argue that hierarchical and market-like transactions are not determined by ownership but by factual control.[140] This variation of traditional TCE is discussed in the debate on a potential new theory of the firm.[141] Although the expansion of the

---

[134] COASE (1937, p.338) argues that "the operation of the market costs something and by forming an organization and allowing some authority (an entrepreneur) to direct the resources, certain marketing costs are saved."
[135] See MCLAREN (2000) for this simple transaction cost model. MCLAREN looks at the impact of economic openness on vertical structure of an economy.
[136] See KLEIN ET AL (1978).
[137] See MCLAREN (2000), p. 1240.
[138] JOSKOW (1988), p. 71.
[139] See RAJAN/ZINGALES (1998a).
[140] See KUMAR ET AL (2001), p. 9. On the one hand, Japanese automobile suppliers are Keiretsu members even though they are separate legal entities. On the other hand, GM's suppliers are divisions of the same firm but face competition with each other. However, there is still a great number of firms for which the legal definition of the firm is the best concept of firm boundaries, see RAJAN/ZINGALES (2000).
[141] See e.g. RAJAN/ZINGALES (1998a, b), RAJAN/ZINGALES (2000), RAJAN/ZINGALES (2001).

TCE framework by these authors can provide fruitful insights, I will use the traditional TCE view according to WILLIAMSON (1985), i.e. the legal definition of a firm as a nexus of contracts, that is more suitable for empirical testing procedures using balance sheet data.

According to TCE the governance mode is a function of the transaction dimensions. The arguments of this function are asset specificity, uncertainty, and frequency. The literature on vertical firm boundaries, e.g. GLOBERMAN (1980), HENNART (1988), LIEBERMAN (1991), has focused to a great extent on these dimensions with asset specificity being the main determinant.

The impact of asset specificity on transaction cost can be modeled using a simple heuristic model following WILLIAMSON (1985). Markets offer low production costs but with increasing asset specificity sequential adaptations to unexpected changes become more and more difficult. This means that negotiations about contractual obligations in situations that are not specified in the contract, i.e. the market-based governance medium, become difficult. Within a hierarchy the integrated transaction partner can be forced to adapt to a change, i.e. management by fiat replaces market-based haggling. The amount of potential haggling increases with certain characteristics of a transaction. The key characteristic of a transaction is asset specificity. Asset specificity is defined as the difference between first best and second best use of an asset in terms of productive value lost.[142] Transaction costs of hierarchies $H(k)$ and of markets $M(k)$ are a function of asset specificity k. Let $H(0) > M(0) > 0$ and $dM/dk > dH/dk$ for all k because of set-up costs etc. for hierarchical coordination. The transaction cost differential is $\Delta TC = H(k) - M(k)$. With increasing asset specificity, the fundamental transformation makes sequential adaptations to unexpected changes more difficult. Hence, hierarchies are the superior governance structure in situations with asset specificity below k' shown in the following figure.

---

[142] See WILLIAMSON (1985), KLEIN ET AL (1978).

Figure 5: Transaction costs

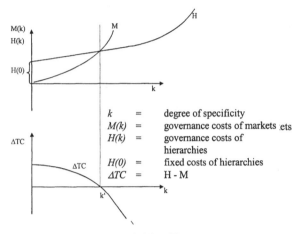

Source: WILLIAMSON (1985), p. 103 and WILLIAMSON (1991), p. 23.

Now, production costs are introduced to the model. According to WILLIAMSON (1985) markets aggregate uncorrelated demands, realize risk-pooling benefits, and avoid many of the bureaucratic hazards. This results in a positive production cost difference compared to hierarchies, ΔPC. The positive cost difference shows the locus of dynamic equilibria with the same output level at different k-values. With increasing asset specificity, ΔPC decreases asymptotically to zero because market benefits are smaller for less standardized goods with a high k-value.

This means for example that the production cost advantages of producing highly specific goods internally are tiny in comparison to their acquisition on the market. The optimum is reached at a critical k-value, k'', that minimizes the sum of ΔTC and ΔPC that is labeled total cost differential (ΔC). ΔC is negative for k-values exceeding k''. The introduction of production costs shifts the critical k-value (efficiency boundary) to the right and extends the market interval compared to the situation without production costs. A graphical representation of the model variables including total cost in the figure below:

Figure 6: Transaction and Production Costs

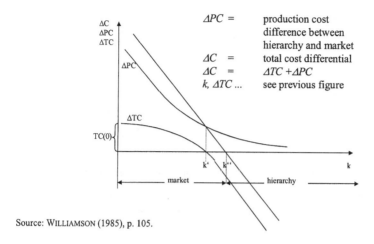

Source: WILLIAMSON (1985), p. 105.

However, all transactions occur in a certain type of transaction environment that influences the optimal governance mode.[143] The institutional setting of a transaction is particularly crucial for the analysis of vertical firm boundaries in an international comparison. Therefore, transaction governance is also a function of the transaction environment. An adequate and appealing conceptual framework to look at the impact of changes in the environment is given in WILLIAMSON (1991).[144] Here, the institutional environment of the firm is explored and integrated into the TCE analysis.[145]

Changes in the environment are modeled as a parametric shift in the variable theta. Theta is a parameter that represents the institutional setting of a transaction that influences the comparative costs of governance. Variance in theta can e.g. result from different institutional environments in which the firm operates. Hence, the cost of governing a transaction can be described as:

---

[143] See BAUR (1990), p. 84.

[144] This setup has e.g. been frequently used in the international business literature. For example, OXLEY (1999) uses and operationalizes this framework to test the impact of different national property rights regimes on the governance mode of international transactions (degree of equity swaps in strategic alliances).

[145] In an agency-theoretical model, GURBAXANI/WHANG (1991) argue that the impact of ICT on governance is highly context-related, i.e. a result of concrete market conditions, industry structure etc. Therefore, the ICT environment and other environmental factors are taken into account.

$$f(k, \theta) = \text{cost of transaction governance,}$$

with k = asset specificity, θ = institutional environment

WILLIAMSON (1991) looks at parameter changes of four kinds: changes in property rights, contract law, reputation effects, and uncertainty.[146] For example, changes in the property rights regime (i.e. protection mechanism for investments in specialized knowledge and information) can induce a parameter shift. In an environment where it is easier that this specialized knowledge is appropriated by rivals, suppliers, and/or customers "vertical or lateral integration into stages of production where the hazards of leakage are greatest is sometimes undertaken".[147] I argue that the ICT environment is a dimension of theta which is not a traditional interpretation of this variable. However, I argue that it is a reasonable and a useful way to understand theta.[148] Thus, I assume that transaction environments, i.e. theta values, vary across different national, temporal, and technological settings.[149] In the following I scrutinize the characteristic determinants of a transaction environment. Here, the transaction cost environment is operationalized with a country.

Using the WILLIAMSON (1991) model, I understand changes in the ICT environment as a parametric shift in theta. New ICT decreases both, the fixed cost and the variable cost of coordinating economic activities.[150] The parameter shift increases the critical asset specificity value where hierarchical governance becomes inferior to market governance in terms of total governance cost, i.e. transaction cost and production cost. Graphically, we can describe the fixed cost reduction as a downward shift of both curves, the market and hierarchy line. This decreases overall governance cost but does not change the critical specificity value where hierarchies are superior to market-based coordination mechanisms. If additional ICT-induced reductions in variable cost are taken into account the proportion of transactions governed by markets increases. We can represent this as a reduction of the curve's slope.[151] The effect can be described in a heuristic governance model as shown in the following figure:

---

[146] See WILLIAMSON (1991), p. 287.
[147] See WILLIAMSON (1991), p. 289-290. See also: TEECE (1986a).
[148] COASE (2002) supports this interpretation in a recent speech by noting that the level of transaction costs is "affected by technological factors."
[149] This understanding of theta is in line with OXLEY (1999) and OXLEY/YEUNG (2001).
[150] PICOT ET AL (1996), p. 70.

Figure 7: Impact of ICT on Firm Boundaries as a Parameter Shift

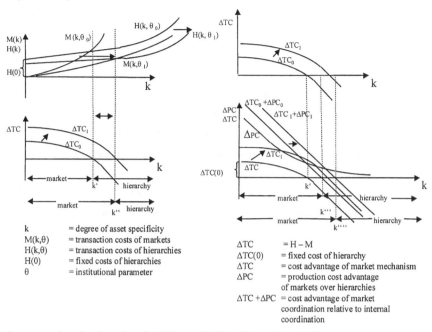

k	= degree of asset specificity
M(k,θ)	= transaction costs of markets
H(k,θ)	= transaction costs of hierarchies
H(0)	= fixed costs of hierarchies
θ	= institutional parameter

ΔTC	= H – M
ΔTC(0)	= fixed cost of hierarchy
ΔTC	= cost advantage of market mechanism
ΔPC	= production cost advantage of markets over hierarchies
ΔTC +ΔPC	= cost advantage of market coordination relative to internal coordination

Source: own figure based on a figure by Williamson (1991), and PICOT ET AL (1996).

The impact of changes in the technological transaction environment (ICT shock) can be shown in the above model. By reducing both fixed and variable transaction cost the slope of both curves becomes less steep in the top left graph. This shifts the intersection of the transaction cost curves in the top left graph to the right. Consequently, the new critical asset specificity value k'' in the bottom left graph shifts to the right. Thereby the proportion of transactions that is governed by markets compared to those governed by hierarchies is raised. The 'move-to-the-market' is based on the assumption that both, fixed and variable transaction costs decline. The two graphs on the right side of the figure show that the inclusion of production cost simply shifts the critical value for k to the right. The ICT shock then shifts k''' to k''''. For the case of rising transaction costs the curves shift to the left.

---

[151] Variable transaction cost are defined as the cost of handling an additional degree of input specificity. The cost of coordinating an ICT-supported transaction that is slightly more complex simply requires the processing of a few more bytes that do not invoke an additional cost, see PICOT ET AL (1996).

The casual empiricism summarized in chapter one indicated that the change in firm boundaries differs between industries. While manufacturing firms appear to have narrower firm boundaries (e.g. outsourcing in the automotive sector) media firms unite large proportions of the media value chain within one firm. In recent years, vertical integration decreased in the manufacturing sector[152] but increased among media firms[153]. The pivotal element that can contribute to our understanding of the differences in the change of corporate organization between the manufacturing and media sector is ICT-induced change in transaction cost and product characteristics. Typical manufacturing products are tangible and can often be traded between firms like commodities. These transactions usually do not require filigree contract solutions to govern these transfer of property rights. In contrast, many media products are involve a high degree of intellectual property rights that are much more difficult to transfer because of product peculiarities analyzed in more detail in the chapter four of this dissertation.

The hypotheses derived from the theory and heuristic modeling in chapter two are subsequently tested in chapter three and four. Chapter three includes an analysis of the manufacturing sector. The hypothesized change in firm boundaries is a 'move-to-the market' as a result of ICT-enabled decreases in transaction costs. Chapter four contains an analysis[154] of ICT as the driver of increasing vertical integration in the media industry. Finally, the results of chapter three and four are compared and summarized in chapter five.

---

[152] See PORTER (1999).
[153] See GARDINI (2002).

3. Changing Firm Boundaries in the Manufacturing Sector

In the following, the outsourcing trend described in the introductory chapter using casual empiricism is viewed in the theoretical context of TCE. Subsequently, I test this trend empirically on a sample of manufacturing sector data. The section is divided in four logical steps. First, ICT impact on firm boundaries is analyzed at the micro-level, i.e. a descriptive portrait of the organizational consequences of different types of ICT is given (part 3.1). Second, I apply the theoretical research design portrayed in chapter 2.5 and thereby link the organizational consequences of ICT to the theories described in the literature (part 3.2). In particular, hypotheses are derived from the heuristic TCE model are derived to describe the ICT-induced changes in transaction governance. Third, the hypotheses developed in part 3.2 are operationalized in order to make them susceptible for empirical analysis (part 3.3). Fourth, two empirical studies – one at the firm level and another at the country level – are performed to examine the ICT impact on firm boundaries (part 3.4 and 3.5 respectively). The chapter ends with a conclusion that summarizes the intermediate findings.

The case examples and the description of the effects of ICT described in the previous chapter together with the survey of the theory might lead us to the presumption that ICT allows for a move towards shrinking firm boundaries, i.e. vertical disintegration.[155] The literature review indicates that there is a number of empirical studies that support this view. However, the existence and the direction of an ICT impact on firm boundaries across countries is not unambiguous and hence remains an empirical question.[156] It has to be answered if variance in firm boundaries is related to differences in the level and/or in the change of ICT variables. Both, a cross-country and a longitudinal comparison could yield some important insights in this context: differences in the development of the ICT environment across countries could help to understand (appropriately controlled for alternative explanations) different firm structures in different environments. Since the ICT environment changed rapidly over time in most countries, I refine the analysis by adding a longitudinal dimension to the cross-country analysis and use panel analysis techniques.

---

[154] The analysis is analyzing the impact of ICT in an indirect way because of difficulties in measuring firm boundary change in the oligopolistically structured media sector. For a detailed description of this analysis see chapter four.

[155] Also hypothesized by PICOT ET AL (2001), p. 407.

[156] Taking into account the literature review, the direction of the impact of ICT on firm boundaries is ambiguous.

Testing international datasets is particularly useful in the context of my research question. The international scope of the analysis originates variance in the institutional settings in which transactions take place. This contributes to the clarification of the fundamental mechanisms that influence the way firms design their organizations. Hence, international business research based on TCE is a fruitful paradigm to understand the factors that shape firm boundaries. The body of TCE research looking at the impact of variation in the environmental conditions on firm boundaries is still growing. The initial theoretical framework for international business research focussing on the environment is given in WILLIAMSON (1991). He introduced a parameter for the institutional conditions under which transactions take place and thereby laid an important foundation for empirical research in international business. The analysis pursued here can provide us with two useful results. First, the role of ICT within the institutional determinants of firm boundaries is clarified. Second, the study can contribute to the improvement of an empirical framework for international business research that is capable of capturing the effects of the ICT dimension (and maybe other dimensions) in the transaction environment.[157]

Before testing the organizational effects of ICT empirically on an aggregate level, I give a brief description about the micro-mechanics of ICT-induced organizational change. This micro-study intends to describe examples of ICTs that can potentially have an organizational impact.

3.1 Organizational Effects of Information and Communication Technology

The phenomenon of ICT-induced changes in organizational structures of firms can be motivated at the micro-level by looking at the development of different types of ICT. I will portrait in brief five types of ICT with regard to their organizational impact in the following paragraphs: supply chain management (SCM) technology, Electronic Data Interchange (EDI), computers with client/server architectures, workflow software, and the Internet.

---

[157] Disintegrating supply chains might become a delicate issue for traditionally closely linked industry structures that exist in Asia. Prominent examples are the Japanese Keiretsu system (a network of shareholding relationships that link manufacturers with their preferred suppliers and retail partners on both ends of the value-chain) or the South-Korean Chaebol, see THE ECONOMIST (2000c). Vertical Keiretsus where producers are linked to suppliers by long-term contracts are common in the Japanese automotive industry, see PFAFFMANN (1998), p. 452. GILSON/ROE (1993), p. 885 argue that Japanese Keiretsus are governance modes with "partial vertical integration through partial cross-ownership, combined with market contracting" However, the focus of this study is not a comparative study of Asian business organization but an explorative examination of firm boundaries in a new ICT environment.

An example how intraorganizational forms of ICT can improve interorganizational coordination is SCM technology. OESTERLE ET AL (2000) defined the goal of SCM to be the process-oriented logistics management by planning and controlling material, information and funds flows using ICT. ELLRAM (1991, p. 14) considered SCM to be the "integrated management approach for planning and controlling the flow of materials from suppliers through the distributions channel to the end user". The ICT involved in the planning process can assume the shape of Enterprise Resource Planning (ERP) software. Via Advanced Planning Systems (ASP)[158], the ERP systems of various members of a supply chain (suppliers, different production plants, distribution centers, points of sale etc.) are connected in order to optimize the interorganizational supply chain coordination. Recently, a committee has been founded with the objective to further improve interorganizational supply chain coordination: the "Collaborative Planning, Forecasting and Replenishment Committee (CPFR)". According to SHERMAN (1998), this concept relies on dynamic information sharing between different business units of a supply chain to create collaborative processes that improves the management of the whole supply chain.

An intraorganizational form that reached a certain penetration level before the Internet achieved its high penetration levels in the late 1990s is EDI. This technology offers a way of exchanging formatted purchase orders and other procurement documents electronically.[159] There is a strong link between this technology and organizational change as stressed by DAVENPORT (1993). NEUBURGER (1994) argues that EDI facilitates organizational change in the form of outsourcing. OESTERLE ET AL (2000, p. 3) notes that EDI was used to integrate the intraorganizational ICTs[160] with suppliers and customers during the 1990s. The interorganizational linkages were predominantly 1:1 links. According to OESTERLE ET AL (2000), future interorganizational links, e.g. provided by Internet applications, will be n:m links. He argues that this would lead to a network structure in which multiple internal and external business units interact.

A form of ICT that was available in the mid 1990s and facilitated non-hierarchical governance structures is the 'client/server architecture' as denoted by PICOT ET AL (2001, p.

---

[158] Sometimes also referred to as Advanced Planning and Scheduling, see. OESTERLE ET AL (2000), p. 324.
[159] EDI transactions are carried out over proprietary networks, usually run by third-party service providers. It can be understood as machine-readable electronic message with standardized content specifying business-to-business orders and requests. See NEUBURGER (1994) for an overview.

51). Client/server ICT[161] was first used in the early 1980s and supports decentralized firm structures via creating interoperability. PICOT ET AL (2001) describe several possible applications of client/server type ICT that create interoperability: an important exemplary application is database management in the form of distributed query processing where several clients (workstations) collectively use a database (e.g. on CD-Rom) on a central server. Hence, client/server ICT provide the information infrastructure to create decentralized organizational structures.

Workflow software is another example of ICT that enhances the efficiency of modular and decentralized firm structures. The main organizational impact of ICT in the form of workflow software and workflow systems lies in its ability to avoid media conversions. This means that order processing can be executed without editing data into the intrafirm ICT because the order is received electronically.[162] Examples are document management systems that support business processes. According to PALERMO/MCCREADY (1992) there are two major groups of workflow software: transaction-oriented and ac-hoc-oriented systems. Transaction oriented systems have predefined process sequences that do not allow user intervention. Ad-hoc-oriented systems allow the intervention of users and the redefinition of specific workflow structures. The use of a specific type of workflow structure depends mainly upon the projected time horizon of a process.[163]

The last and most important form of ICT that affects firm boundaries is the Internet. The Internet provides a technical standard for the communication (the protocol TCP/IP) and presentation (e.g. in HTML[164]) of data.[165] OESTERLE ET AL (2000) found that by using the same business standard, the communication between firms involves no longer much more effort than communication between different departments of the same firm. This fact contributes to the technical feasibility of decentralized firm structures.[166]

All forms of ICT portrayed here can enable organizational change. I will use the Internet as a proxy for the development of an ICT environment in which firms do business. Before the

---

[160] E.g. ERP systems.
[161] A survey on ICT with client/server architectures is given in GEIHS (1995).
[162] See HASENKAMP ET AL (1994).
[163] See PICOT ET AL (2001).
[164] Hypertext Markup Language.
[165] See OESTERLE ET AL (2000).

relationship between ICT and organizational change is investigated empirically I will use the theoretical TCE framework of WILLIAMSON (1991) to derive testable hypotheses.

3.2   Theoretical Research Design and Hypothesis Formulation

In the theoretical framework of WILLIAMSON (1991), ICT-enabled decreases in transaction cost would lead to ceteris paribus more market governance. We would expect transactions in institutional settings with a high availability of external or market coordination mechanisms provided by ICT to be less hierarchical. I conjecture that firms in countries with more developed ICT environments are less vertically integrated and hence have narrower firm boundaries (hypothesis 1). Additionally, I hypothesize that increases in the availability of ICT are associated with decreasing degrees of vertical integration and shrinking firm boundaries (hypothesis 2). The latter hypothesis means that for firms that used to be vertically integrated outsourcing becomes an efficient organizational response to the increased availability of ICT. This leads to the following two hypotheses:

H1: Firms in countries with high levels of ICT development show - ceteris paribus - on average narrow firm boundaries (cross-sectional dimension).

H2: Firms in countries with improving ICT development show - ceteris paribus - on average shrinking firm boundaries (longitudinal dimension).

The literature lacks an empirical analysis of the role ICT plays in international differences in firm structure. As presented before, there is a theoretical motivation[166] and there is evidence[168] in the literature that ICT affects industrial organization. However, the existing literature is not unambiguous but tends to gravitate towards the assessment that increasing availability of ICT allows for more market governance at least in the manufacturing sector.[169] My analysis should

---

[166] PICOT ET AL (2001), p.142-195.
[167] See e.g. MALONE ET AL (1987), CLEMONS ET AL (1993), HOLLAND/LOCKETT (1997).
[168] See e.g. KAMBIL (1991), BRYNJOLFSSON ET AL (1994), HITT (1998).
[169] The impact of ICT on ex-post transaction cost (hold up costs) is not neglected. The ex-ante non-contractibility of excluding a ex-post haggling over quasi-rents is a result of opportunistically exploiting incomplete contracts primarily in small-number situations. ICT affects several elements of this problem like number of transaction partners, opportunism, and contract incompleteness which is shown further below. The overall result (magnitude and direction of the effect) remains an empirical question addressed in this piece of research.

be understood as a new approach to test the 'move-to-the-market' prediction on an international level. The following chapter operationalizes the hypotheses.[170]

3.3   Operationalization

I explore different paths to pursue the desired analysis: (i) a cluster analysis using Euclidean distances to form three groups of ICT environments in which average vertical integration of firms belonging to this group is analyzed, and (ii) an aggregate approach using firm level financial data from Compustat that is aggregated to the country level and examined in a panel analysis.

Both approaches use firm data from the Compustat Global Industrial/Commercial database to construct the firm boundaries measures. To exclude industry effects, I focus on the manufacturing sector.

My empirical analysis uses two principal empirical research designs. The first design is an analysis at the firm level to detect differences in the degree of vertical integration in countries with different ICT environments. Therefore, I look at differences in firm boundary variables across countries with different levels of ICT penetration. The second approach develops the findings from my first analysis further by looking at the causes of the expected differences. In a panel regression design, I analyze vertical integration at the country level and regress these variables against appropriately controlled country-measures of ICT development.

3.3.1   Variables

To test these hypotheses, I develop a firm structure variable that is used as a dependent variables in my analysis.

Dependent Variables

The goal of the analysis is to rationalize observed changes in firm boundaries. The principal dimensions of firm boundaries are firm size and vertical integration. Using TCE as the principal theoretical framework I focus on vertical integration. Vertical Integration has been operationalized in the literature

---

[170] The aggregate level of analysis (firm data is aggregated to the country level) might create some noise in the variables, but adds a lot of insight by providing some interesting institutional variance.

(i)   via a measure for value-added derived from historical financial statements (to determine the degree of vertical integration),[171] as used by ADELMAN (1955), LAFFER (1969), TUCKER/WILDER (1977), LEVY (1985), SPILLER (1985), KERKVLIET (1991), SHIN (2002),

(ii)   via SIC-classified M&A data[172] isolating vertical integration activity,

(iii)   via computing a vertical integration index from input-output tables like in MADDIGAN (1981), and LAWSON/TESKE (1994), or similarly, by counting the number of production stages, like ARMOUR/TEECE (1980), or

(iv)   following FEENSTRA/HANSON (1997) using a distance measure (log distance of manufacturer to nearest upstream and downstream firm with which the manufacturer has a business relationship).[173]

To analyze vertical integration I chose a value-added measure. Value-added seems to be a fair, widely accepted and frequently used measure for the degree of vertical integration and has been used for this purpose throughout the literature.[174]

There is no standardized method to measure value-added.[175] To determine the amount of value-added per firm several approaches coexist in the literature.[176] A potentially viable but unfeasible approach could be re-computing value-added from the amount of value-added tax paid by the respective firm.[177] Apart from the tax recalculation method, there are two basic approaches to determine value-added, a fact that is often referred to as the "dichotomy of value-added".[178] The two approaches are the subtractive and the additive approach:

---

[171] The index structure is the prevailing methodology to measure value-added, see PICOT (1991).

[172] One important driver of recent M&A activity has been technological change and technological convergence (see for the media sector: BALDWIN ET AL (1995), COLLIS ET AL (1997), GREENSTEIN/KHANNA (1997), MASUD (1998), TSENG/LITMAN (1998). However, a problem in the analysis of M&A data is that it seems to occur in waves, i.e. there is autocorrelation in the longitudinal analysis, see BARKOULAS ET AL (2001). Agency cost might also contribute some distortions to this variable.

[173] Spatial proximity is used as a proxy for site specificity in terms of collocation decisions.

[174] See also: BUZELL/GALE (1989), p. 138. There is also a substantive body of German origin literature: PICOT (1991), p. 337, ZAEPFEL (1989), p. 132, LEHMANN (1954), p. 24, MATJE (1994).

[175] Some companies report value-added figures. Due to the lack of standardization of these value-added statements they provide very little additional information for an international comparison, see HALLER/STOLLOWY (1998), p. 47.

[176] Because of the lack of standardization, opinions regarding the definition of value-added do deviate to some extent. For example, VOLLMUTH (1998) considers its components to be personnel expenses, accruals, net interest expenses, net tax payments, plus profit.

[177] The problem is that Global Vantage firms contain a large amount of missing data in this section which severely reduces the quality of the data for this variable.

[178] LEHMANN (1954), p. 11.

(i)   subtractive method: value-added consists of the difference between the value of production and purchased inputs such that

$$Value\text{-}added_{Subtractive\ Method} = Value\ of\ Production^{179} - Purchased\ Inputs$$

The subtractive approach is defined as the difference between value of production, i.e. the sum of sales plus change in inventories (ending inventory less beginning inventory) on the one side and raw materials plus merchandise on the other side. For Global Vantage firms value-added can be defined as 'net total sales less the cost associated with the purchase or depletion of inventories/stocks of raw materials, supplies, and merchandise'. The second method is the additive method:

(ii)   additive method: value-added is determined by the sum of all remunerations of all value-contributing productive factors such that

$$Value\text{-}added_{Additive\ Method} = \Sigma\ value\text{-}contributing\ productive\ factors$$

Value-added according to the additive method is equal to the sum of all remunerations of employees, governments, and capital providers (equity and debt providers) plus not appropriated income (retained earnings). This shows that value-added is the amount of all partial values added by the totality of a firm's stakeholders that accrues either as cost or income. Usually this is represented as follows:

Table 1: Distribution of Value-added

Appropriation of Value-added	Costs Added	(+ Income)[180]
Share of the employees	Wages and salaries, incl. social welfare expenditure	(+ Employee profit sharing)
Capital providers' share	Financial expenses [=> Cost of capital]	(+ Dividends + Interests) [=> Return on investment]
Government's share	Taxes and similar expenses (excluding income taxes)	(+ Income taxes)
Enterprise's share (corporate share)	Calculated charges (depreciation, amortization and write back)	(+ Retained earnings)

Source: HALLER/STOLOWY (1998), p. 49.

---

[179] Value of production = net sales + change in inventories.
[180] The column "Income" is redundant because usually cost items can be expressed as income items, e.g. return of investment (investor's perspective) can be expressed as cost of capital (firm's perspective).

TUCKER/WILDER (1977, p. 86) use an additive approach with the following items:

depreciation and amortization

+ fixed charges (interest expense)

+ labor and related expense

+ pension and retirement expense

+ incentive compensation expense

+ income taxes

+ net income (after taxes)

<u>+ rental expense</u>

= value-added

Having operationalized vertical integration I formulate a value-added index to proxy vertical integration of the form

VAI = Value-added Index (VAI) = Value-Added / Total Sales

Using Compustat/Global Vantage items the indices are computed as follows: I follow BRESNAHAN ET AL (2002) by using a specification of value-added as the sum of operating income and staff expense. Value-added is equated as the difference between total sales (Item #1) and materials. Materials is calculated by subtracting staff expenses (Item #42) from total expense. Total expense was computed as the difference between Operating Income Before Depreciation (Item #14) and Net Sales. Hence, value-added is the sum of operating income and staff expense.[181]

An alternative specification is the subtractive view. Therefore, Global Vantage items #1 (Net Sales) minus #6 (Raw Materials, Supplies, and Merchandise) could be used. This measure is highly correlated with the additive specification. Due to richer data, I use the additive specification.

The rationale for the indicator VAI becomes clear by looking at the subtractive definition of value-added. Rising values of direct input factors (i.e. 'raw materials, supplies, and merchandise') means that less value is added in the observed value chain segment (i.e.

---

[181] This shows the duality of value-added mentioned above.

firm).[182] Backward integration tends to reduce the purchases of material inputs while sales are supposed to remain unchanged resulting in a higher value-added ratio. Integrating forward into distribution tends to increase sales more than proportionally to purchased inputs leading to higher value-added values and vice versa.[183] The rational for the additive version of VAI is analogous.

The index structure takes out the monetary dimension and makes this measure comparable across countries without running into exchange-rate and purchasing power parity problems in terms of comparability. It will be close to one in the case of high vertical integration, i.e. for firms that rarely call upon third parties. The index is close to zero for firms that add only marginal value to their purchased inputs.

A potential distortion of my measure is the argument that the value-added measurement of firm structure is affected by performance impacts. In the same manner, outsourcing could be interpreted as a defensive measure for troubled firms to cut cost. There are two defenses to this allegation. First, I want to take a governance perspective and thereby focus exclusively on firm structure variables abstracting from performance measures. Firms that change their boundaries for performance reasons are only adapting their organization to the most efficient organizational mode.

Second and more important, TUCKER/WILDER (1977) constructed a modified value-added measure as it is used here. Then they compared the original measure with one that had been corrected for profits in the numerator and denominator. The results were not affected significantly.

Other distortions of the dependent variable are non-equity/"invisible" changes in firm boundaries via new organizational forms or hybrids (e.g. strategic alliances, firm networks, long-term contracts etc.). Hybrids face operationalization limitations and can be analyzed better using questionnaire-based research compared to financial statement data. Due to the

---

[182] The increased value of direct inputs stems by assumption from upstream firms that added value to the inputs purchased by the observed firm. Increased value might stem from price and/or quantity increases. If the value of direct inputs decreases we assume that the respective firm increased its vertical integration and is now performing an additional value-adding activity upstream itself instead of purchasing the input.
[183] See TUCKER/WILDER (1977), p. 83.

aggregate level of my analysis and the financial statement data I use these quasi-integration solutions remain still unobserved here.

Although value-added is a frequently used measure, it is susceptible to a bias when it is used along an industry value-chain because the amount of value-added decreases along the value chain from upstream to downstream.[184] This bias is significantly reduced by following LEVY (1985) and restricting the sample to manufacturing firms in order to get comparable figures. I avoid this bias by restricting myself to the manufacturing industries (SIC Codes 2xxx-3xxx).[185] The set of dependent variables is regressed against a number of independent variables that are described in the following paragraphs.

Independent Variables

For the sake of avoiding the missing variable problem[186] explanatory variables derived from all theories summarized in the second chapter are included in the estimation equation.

The independent variable of central interest is ICT. The main goal is to find an appropriate operationalization of the 'information and communication environment'. The variable should focus on the interorganizational dimension of ICT and reflect the totality of ICTs that facilitates coordination across firm boundaries.

I assume that the rise of Internet facilities is positively associated with the ICT development of a country. Therefore, the dispersion and development of the Internet is used as an operationalization for the ICT environment. I follow OXLEY/YEUNG (2001) to measure the ICT environment. The development and dissemination of ICT is measured by the number of Internet hosts per capita (ICTI). The reason to chose Internet penetration is that the change in the ICT environment is captured best by a broad measure. Changes and innovations in ICT have always occurred, but the 1990s showed a rapidly changing ICT landscape with the emergence of the Internet. I further assume that this type of ICT affects inter-firm coordination especially in a vertical sense, i.e. communication with suppliers, recently also with end-consumers (via online selling techniques). Another crucial advantage is that Internet

---

[184] See LEVY (1985), p. 440, TUCKER/WILDER (1977), p. 83.

[185] This is the usual definition of the manufacturing sector, see e.g. SHAVER/FLYER (2000), p.14.

[186] By omitting an important independent variable, the OLS estimates are not BLUEs (i.e. best linear unbiased estimators). On the other hand, adding too many variables creates noise to the analysis. The optimal model setup achieves a balance between these two effects.

hosts and user statistics show a high degree of international comparability relative to firm level ICT data, e.g. the firm's IT budget.

In addition to the two variables focussing on information technology, two variables measuring the communication environment are used to obtain a comprehensive picture of the ICT environment: the number of phone lines (ICTP) and the amount of telecommunication investment per country (ICTT). The spread of basic telecommunication facilities (here proxied by ICTP and ICTT) is expected to reflect the advances in communication technology that also facilitates interorganizational coordination.[187] All ICT variables are portrayed in detail in appendix II.

Organizational theories of firm boundaries relate differences in vertical integration to different levels of asset specificity k. Firms with high ratios of intangibles are likely to be more vertically integrated than others due to higher asset specificity.[188] A good measure of asset specificity is the R&D intensity in a particular country.[189] I include both, an aggregated measure for R&D as a proportion of GDP and a firm-level measure constructed from financial statement data of the sample firms. I use a variable with ratio structure to simplify international comparison.[190]

---

[187] In recent years, we can observe a process of blurring the boundaries between the different streams of technology -like telecommunication, media, and information technology- that is often referred to as "convergence", i.e. previously distinct technologies and industries merge by sharing similar technological platforms, see WIRTZ (2001, p. 4). Therefore, I will use the term information and communication technology (ICT) that subsumes all different means of advances information processing and communication. ICT should be defined as the totality of electronic means to capture, process, store, and communicate information.

[188] See LEVY (1985), p. 439. The argument is that research intensive industries tend to use specialized inputs because non-standardized physical inputs are often procured when new products and new technologies emerge. Additionally, research intensive firms are supposed to have human capital that is used transaction-specific (i.e. special research teams). Using the same logic MORCK/YEUNG (1991) argue that firms with high ratios of intangibles are rewarded by the stock market (measured by changes in their Tobin's q) when they internationalize using FDI (the hierarchical vehicle) and not a market-based form (e.g. licensing or exporting). This is a central empirical finding that supports the internalization theory, see CALVET (1981), RUGMAN (1986), TEECE (1986b), CASSON (1987), MORCK/YEUNG (1991), BUCKLEY/CASSON (1991).

[189] Asset specificity is often proxied by R&D over sales or over total assets, see e.g. ZECKHAUSER/POUND (1990).

[190] The ratio structure is the prevailing structure of R&D intensity measures and is a common proxy for intangible assets in firms that drive internalization and hierarchical governance, e.g. MORCK/YEUNG (1991). Advertising intensity is another usual proxy to measure product differentiation. The degree of product differentiation found with the products sold by a particular firm is supposed to be positively related to vertical integration. Again, the transmission mechanism is supposed to be asset specificity. The reason is that non-standardized inputs are frequently used in firms with differentiated products. Unfortunately, there is no advertising figure in the Global Vantage database because international comparability would be too low.

I would expect firms with high R&D expenditure to be more vertically integrated (e.g. component suppliers integrating forward into final assembly) because of asset specificity. The reason is that integration is used to protect innovation. Innovations are public goods and therefore face free rider problems.[191] These rents run the risk of private appropriations. Firm boundaries are drawn and determined by the extent to which these intangibles are safeguarded against potential dissipation through leakages.[192]

Variance in capital intensity is another determinant of firm boundaries, especially vertical integration. KUMAR ET AL (2001) find that capital intensity is positively related to firm boundaries. I use the average number of employees per total assets (TAS_EMP) to account for differences in capital intensity.[193]

Differences in vertical integration might also be related to differences in asset management. I include the total asset turnover (SA_BY_AS), i.e. net total sales divided by net total assets, to control for differences in asset management, productivity and efficiency.[194]

As suggested by *institutional theories* of firm boundaries, the institutional framework of a country is a likely determinant of firm boundaries.[195] This variable corresponds to the a dimension of theta, i.e. the political environment in which a firm operates.[196] The political environment determines the quality of the procedure if and how rules on transaction governance and the exchange of property rights are modified. The quality of this procedure is supposed to be related to the degree of separation of powers. For example, in systems with a high degree of separation of powers there are sufficient checks and balances to limit the actions of the agenda setter, i.e. the executive.

A reliable and valid measure of this likelihood is presumably the POLCON index[197] that is also available as panel data. Since autocracies are characterized by low POLCON scores high POLCON score indicate sound institutional design. As described in the theoretical research

---

[191] See SAMUELSON (1954), and MUSGRAVE (1959). Public goods are portrayed in chapter 4 in more detail.
[192] WILLIAMSON (1985), p. 45.
[193] Employees over total assets is a common proxy for capital intensity, see LEHAMANN/WEIGAND (2000).
[194] This might also capture undesired residual industry effects and differences in efficiency that influence the degree of vertical integration
[195] See LUNN (1985), pp. 423, YU (1981), pp. 234.
[196] HARM (2001) stresses the importance of the political environment in international business research.
[197] See HENISZ (2002).

review there are two rivaling expectations regarding the sign of this regressor. Knowing that financial markets in political systems with sound institutional design are usually more developed we expect a positive correlation between our firm boundary measures and the POLCON index.[198] Assuming that sound legal systems allow for a better use of the market mechanism and signify less dependency on internal coordination would lead to ceteris paribus more market governance.

Alternative variables to measure the political environment including intellectual property rights protection and the rule of law that can be fitted into the model are the LA PORTA-Index, see LA PORTA ET AL (1998), and the PriceWaterhouseCoopers (PWC) index of country opacity.[199] Both are only available as cross-sectional data at a single point in time. Therefore, I chose the POLCON index as the principal political variable.

The overall market size of the analyzed countries is a determinant of firm boundaries as suggested by *technological theories* of firm size.[200] Proxies for market size that are frequently used are total population or total GDP. I use GDP because it proxies the economic size of the market better than the number of people living in a country.[201]

Additionally, I include the annual average rate of inflation as an important control because it is a good measure of the ability of a currency to represent stable value in contracting.[202] Furthermore, I use a number of other control variables. The ratio of exports over GDP is included in the regression equation to account for differences in the degree of openness between different countries. It is reasonable to assume that openness of an economy has an impact on cross-border out- and insourcing decisions. Since cross-border (vertical) mergers seem to be easier in open economies, firms in open economies are expected to be more vertical integrated. GDP per capita will be used to account for income- and wealth-related differentials between countries. Following the line of reasoning that firms in countries with

---

[198] See chapter 2.1 for the discussion about the expected sign of this variable.

[199] Opacity is defined by PWC as the lack of clear, accurate, formal, easily discernible, and widely accepted practices in the broad arena where business, finance, and government meet and can be expressed as an opacity risk premium for bond issues denominated in basis points, see PRICEWATERHOUSECOOPERS (2001).

[200] See STIGLER (1951).

[201] I argue that population figures are less meaningful in my analysis because they focus on the demographic size and not so much on the economic size of a country. The latter matters for the organizational decision of a firm trying to gain market share.

[202] See BECK ET AL (2002), p. 12. According to WU/ZHANG (2001) both, the number of firms and each firm's size is reduced by inflation. Hence, the overall impact on average firm size per country is unclear.

developed political regimes and more developed financial markets have better growth opportunities, I expect a positive relationship between development measured by GDP per capita and vertical integration. In order to focus on vertical firm size, I include general firm size variables to eclipse firm size as a determinant. Since firm size can not be ruled out as a determinant of vertical integration, I apply common firm size measures, i.e. average sales, average total assets, and average number of employees.[203]

To account for the important role of corporate governance in designing an organization with efficient firm boundaries I add ownership concentration as a dummy variable, HIGH_CON, representing a frequently used corporate governance variable. FRANKS/MAYER (1994) found that ownership concentration is associated with a higher turnover of directors in Germany. There are several findings supporting that large shareholders play an active role in corporate governance. For Germany, FRANKS/MAYER (1994) found that large shareholders are associated with higher turnover of directors. In Japan, KAPLAN/MINTON (1994) analyzed the Japanese case and discover that firms with large shareholders are more likely to dismiss managers of under-performing firms. The empirical studies show that ownership concentration can avoid the free rider problem. In a world of increasing availability of ICT, I expect a negative relationship between ownership concentration and vertical integration: apathy to efficiently adapt the boundaries of the firm, i.e. to implement a slimmer organizational structure, should be more common in situations with low levels of ownership concentration.

3.3.2 The Data

The data is taken from the Compustat/Global Vantage 'Global Industrial/Commercial' database containing historical financial statements of listed companies in a number of countries. A common objection to cross-country analyses is the existence of *industry effects*, i.e. the fact that there is a bias in the data due to significant differences in the observations between industries, especially between the service and the manufacturing sector. This effect is controlled for by selecting a firm sample from the manufacturing sector and study it in different countries. I also control for capital intensity that often is a characteristic of a particular industry because of related production processes. A narrower industry definition

---

[203] All three variable represent common proxies for firm size, see BRYNJOLFSSON ET AL (1994).

would potentially filter out more industry effects but surely reduce the number of firms that are used to compute country aggregate figures. The industry effects are supposed to be most evident between the service and the manufacturing sector. By excluding service firms and other industries that might bias the analysis like utilities (usually high public sector influence) and financial institutions (different balance sheet structure) I notably reduce distortions from industry effects. Data quality in terms of observations per country average is more valuable than filtering out slightly more industry effects. Therefore I use a broader manufacturing industry definition.

The selection of countries to be compared is biased towards industrialized countries for the following reason: ICT induced organizational change is supposed to take place primarily in the US and Europe. Rich countries account for only 15% of the world's population but 90% of global IT spending and 80% of Internet users.[204] The homogeneity of the sample compared to a mixed sample from OECD and less developed countries (LDCs) is strongly desired for comparability reasons. The ICT variables include sufficient variation to isolate the impact of ICT from other firm boundary determinants. The timeframe is chosen in order to capture the time interval in which ICT environment changed most.[205]

3.4   Empirical Research Design I: Firm Level

In a first step, I analyze the degree of vertical integration at the firm level. The goal is to check if firms in countries with high degrees of ICT development have different firm boundaries compared to firms in low ICT countries.

3.4.1   Descriptive Statistics

I use the Compustat Global Industrial/Commercial Database[206] to construct my firm boundary measure. The analysis is restricted to manufacturing firms for comparability reasons. I take all firms with SIC Code 2xxx –3xxx and eliminate from 50,874 firm years all firm years without values for 1990-2000 for the data items: #1 Sales, #6 Raw Materials, # 14 Operating Income, #42 Staff Expense, # 52 Research and Development Expense, # 89 Total Assets, #162

---

[204] See THE ECONOMIST (2000d).
[205] TCT/IP-based ICT like the Internet emerged as a major phenomenon in the early 1990s.
[206] Formerly known as Global Vantage.

Number of Employees.[207] This data selection routine allows a computation of the vertical integration measure for 559 firms.[208] I test if firms in different ICT environments in terms of ICT penetration show significant differences in vertical integration.

We can observe variance in the ICT environment both across countries and over time. A descriptive statistic of the actual ICT penetration mean from 1991 to 2000 displays that ICT penetration rises over time. Geographically, the Scandinavian countries (especially Finland, Norway, and Sweden) and the USA have high levels of ICT per capita. Low ICT penetration can be observed e.g. in Spain, Italy, Portugal, and South Africa as shown in the figure below.

Figure 8: Number of Internet Hosts per Million Inhabitants and per Year

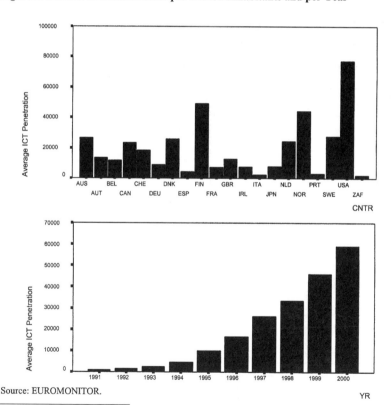

Source: EUROMONITOR.

---

[207] The appendix III contains definitions of the items used.
[208] These countries include Australia (AUS), Austria (AUT), Belgium (BEL), Canada (CAN), Switzerland (CHE), Germany (DEU), Denmark (DNK), Spain (ESP), Finland (FIN), France (FRA), Great Britain (GBR), Ireland (IRL), Italy (ITA), Japan (JPN), The Netherlands (NLD), Norway (NOR), Portugal (PRT), Sweden (SWE), United States of America (USA), South Africa (ZAF).

3.4.2 Empirical Model Specifications

In order to analyze firm data regarding the impact of the ICT environment I use a dummy variable approach. Therefore I codify country-years from 1991 to 2000 into three levels of ICT development characterizing three different ICT environments, i.e. low, medium and high ICT development. I use a hierarchical cluster analysis[209] with Euclidean distances to split the country-years into three clusters of country-years in terms of ICT penetration level. The alternative would be to use cutoff-values and/or n-tiles. The advantage of using cluster analysis instead of mere cutoff-values is that the mechanism is designed to find groups of country-years with high internal homogeneity and high external heterogeneity. This means that comparability of country-years is very high.[210] The cluster analysis gives me three groups that consist of country-years. Hence, I receive the following ICT dummy variable:

ICT_L: high (3), medium (2), and low (1) level of ICT development/penetration

Table 2: Codification of ICT Environments: Internet Penetration

No. of country years	*ICT Development (Internet hosts and users per capita) (1=low, 2=medium, 3 = high)*						
Country	1	2	3	year	1	2	3
AUS	7	2	1	1991	20		
AUT	8	2		1992	20		
BEL	9	1		1993	20		
CAN	7	2	1	1994	20		
CHE	8	2		1995	20		
DEU	8	2		1996	19	1	
DNK	7	2	1	1997	16	4	
ESP	9	1		1998	13	7	
FIN	5	3	2	1999	6	11	3
FRA	10			2000	3	11	6
GBR	8	2		Total	157	34	9
IRL	8	2		n = 200			
ITA	9	1					
JPN	8	2					
NLD	8	2					
NOR	6	2	2				
PRT	10						
SWE	6	2	2				
USA	6	4					
ZAF	10						
Total	157	34	9				

---

[209] See TRYON (1939).
[210] Cluster analysis minimizes the average of all possible distances of all possible pairs within a cluster. Therefore, they are a useful technique to form three coherent groups of ICT penetration in terms of Internet hosts per capita and Internet user per capita. This explains the non-membership of the USA in cluster (3): Scandinavian countries have higher ICT penetration when both, Internet hosts and Internet users are taken into account simultaneously.

Although there is a lack of data for the ICT variables in 1990 it is reasonable to assume ICT development level 1 (low) for all countries. The vast majority of firm years is in category 1 as shown in the following figure:

Figure 9: Distribution of Country Years in Terms of ICT Penetration

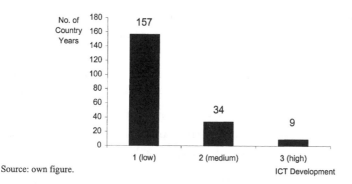

Source: own figure.

3.4.3 Results and Discussion

The results are not contradictory to the interpretation that firms with low levels of vertical integration are found especially in highly developed ICT environments. A graphical representation of average vertical integration in the respective country-years is given in following figure:

Figure 10: Average Vertical Integration by ICT Penetration Group

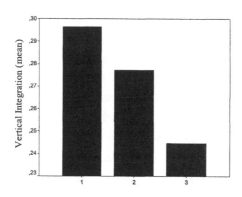

Source: own figure.

ICT Development (1=low, 2=medium, 3=high)

67

The graphic gives us the impression that ICT penetration is negatively related to the degree of vertical integration. In firm-years with low Internet penetration the mean value for vertical integration measured with the additive method was between 29% and 30%. Firms in medium ICT penetration years had on average a vertical integration index score of nearly 28% (roughly 25% for ICT_L score 3). This is tentative evidence for a negative relationship between ICT development of a country in a particular year and the organization of its firms in this particular year. However, it is still to be unclear if the differences are significant.

The vertical integration firm-level measure does not seem to be normally distributed. A Kolmogorov-Smirnov-Test values was not significant at the 5% level. Hence, non-parametric test procedures are applied. A Kruskal-Wallis-Test supports the impression gained from the last figure: the three clusters of country-years differ significantly in terms of vertical integration measured on a 1% confidence level (two-tailed).[211]

Table 3: Rank Test for Vertical Integration

	ICT-Level	N	Average Rank
vertical integration [%]	1	463	288,65
	2	76	248,53
	3	20	199,30
	Sum	559	

	VAI
Chi-Square	9.206
df	2
p	0.010***

*** significant on the 1% confidence level (2-tailed test)

The descriptive statistics confirm the suggestion that ICT negatively affects vertical integration. Due to the structure of the analysis a cluster of country-years can contain both, 'late' country-years from countries with slow ICT development during the 1990s and 'early' years from countries with fast ICT development. Obviously, there are country-factors affecting the vertical integration variable that have to be taken into account. To comprehend the mechanics of ICT impact on vertical integration a multivariate analysis of ICT in association with alternative determinants of firm boundaries is necessary. This analysis is pursued in the following paragraphs.

3.5 Empirical Research Design II: Country Level

3.5.1 Descriptive Statistics

I use the two vertical integration indices described above. In addition to the ICT environment I look at alternative determinants of firm boundaries. A description of the various dependent and independent variables is given in appendix IV. The descriptive statistics are displayed in the table below.

Data is available for 20 countries over the years 1990 to 1997 for most variables except vertical integration.[212] Vertical integration is analyzed for 14 countries and 7 years (1991 to 1997) in a dataset without missing values.[213] I omitted all firms without consistently reported data for this period in order to avoid a bias that results from entry and exit of firms from/into the sample.[214]

Table 4: Descriptive Statistics (Country Years)

Variable	Min	Max	Mean	SD
VAI (vertical integration index)	0.1516	0.4753	0.2652	0.0534
ICTIPC (Internet hosts per capita)	2.7040	9488.886	799.1066	1448.1163
ICTPPC (telephone lines per capita)	272.760	662.020	484.83347	91.28144
ICTTPC (teco inv pc)	247.946	17747.349	3178.79198	3753.20810
LNINF (Inflation rate, log of)	-0.6539	2.4292	0.930482	0.552035
EXPGDP (exports as a proportion of GDP)	0.109	0.817	.30833	0.16583
POLCON	0.173	0.708	.47218	0.12090
AS (Average Total Sales)	4.7165	3527.1047	1335.490	1073.33256
ATA (Average Total Assets)	4.0583	3984.2944	1381.5610	1078.86175
GDP (Gross Domestic Product)	49.4583	2419.3008	557.740457	602.354361
GDP_PC (Gross Domestic Product per capita)	0.008	0.044	0.00229	0.000744
TAS_ EMP (total assets per employee)	0.074	14.529	2.33889	3.65796
LN_ANOE (average no. of employees, log of)	0.0942	3.7390	1.916123	0.805460
RDSAAV (R&D investment over total sales)	0	0.0335	0.000835	0.0007815

[211] In order to focus on the years with high variance in the ICT environment I modified the timeframe for the analysis by eliminating all firm-years prior to 1995 and re-performing the Kruskal-Wallis-Test. The differences between the three groups are still significant on the 5% confidence level (2-tailed test).
[212] In contrast to general firm boundaries measures (employees, total sales, total assets), vertical integration data is only available for 7 years and 14 countries.
[213] The countries are: Austria, Belgium, Switzerland, Germany, Denmark, Spain, Finland, France, Great Britain, Ireland, Italy, Netherlands, Norway, Portugal.
[214] The sample construction is described in more detail in the appendix V.

3.5.2 Empirical Model Specifications

Since the analysis of the research question requires both, a temporal dimension and a cross-sectional dimension, models for panel data are applied. The basic framework for this discussion is a regression model of the form[215]

$$y_{it} = \alpha_i + \beta' x_{it} + \varepsilon_{it} \text{ with } i = 1,...,n, \ t = 1,...,T$$

It is assumed that there is an individual effect α_i that is constant over time t and specific to the particular cross-sectional unit i (country), i.e. there is a common slope. There are two possible interpretations of α_i. The choice of the interpretation has some methodological implications and determines if either the random effect (RE) or the fixed-effect (FE) model will be used.[216] The fixed effect model interprets α_i as a cross-section specific constant term while the random effects approach specifies that α_i is a cross-section specific disturbance term. The fixed effect model uses ordinary least squares (OLS) estimation technique while the random effect setup relies on general least squares (GLS).[217]

The models differ mainly in their assumption about the error term. The random effect model assumes that the error term is split into a firm-specific and a general error term assuming that the error of each cross-section unit is uncorrelated with the other regressors.[218] The fact that this assumption might be violated here favors the selection of a FE model. An argument in favor of the fixed effect setup is fact that microdata (individuals or firms) is usually suitable for the random effect model version while cross-country data is usually analyzed using the fixed effect setup.[219]

On the one hand, my cross-country setup seems to require a fixed-effect setup following the argument that cross-country data requires a fixed effect setup. On the other hand, random effects setups are more suitable for data that represents only an excerpt of the total population. This is obviously the case in my data situation. The standard test to determine the appropriate

---

[215] For reference regarding the general empirical research design using panel data see GREENE (2000), p. 557-589.

[216] The two type of models represent two ways to capture cross-sectional heterogeneity, see GREENE (2000).

[217] See GREENE (2000), chapter 14.

[218] See GREENE (2000) and KENNEDY (1998), p. 227.

[219] See BALTAGI (1995).

panel data model, i.e. the Hausman test[220], will be performed to receive some additional information for this decision. To sum it up, the answer to the question which model should be applied is ambivalent.

A drawback of the FE setup is the loss of degrees of freedom while the RE setup needs the restrictive assumption that the unobservable effects are uncorrelated with regressors.[221] JUDGE ET AL (1985) argue that the violation of this assumption leads to biased and inconsistent estimates. The FE model is a classical regression model and can be specified as follows:

$$y_i = i\, \alpha_i + X_i\, \beta + \varepsilon_i$$

with y_i and X_i being the T observations[222] for the i-th unit (country), ε_i being the vector of disturbances, and α_i is an unknown parameter to be estimated.[223] Using dummy variables leads us to

$$y = D\alpha + X\beta + \varepsilon$$

where d_i is a dummy variable indicating the i-th unit (country or year) and D is a (nT)xn matrix $D = [d_1, d_2, \ldots, d_n]$.

The FE model uses dummy variables for the N-1 countries. The analysis can be extended via introducing fixed time effects which adds another T-1 dummy variable to the analysis leading to (n-1)+(T-1) dummies.[224] One of the time effects and one of the group effects has to be dropped to avoid perfect collinearity. Since year specific effects are not very likely the 'time specific effects' set of dummies might be omitted to save degrees of freedom.[225] A major drawback of the fixed effect specification is the number of degrees of freedom lost. This

---

[220] The Hausman specification test has been developed by HAUSMAN (1978). He found that the results derived from the fixed-effect specification of a panel regression model are significantly different from the results generated with a random-effects specification in his analysis of Michigan income dynamics. Based on his findings he developed a test method to indicate the appropriate setup.

[221] There is a ongoing debate over the appropriateness of panel data models. Some authors consider the FE model superior to the usually biased RE model, see GRILICHES (1984), p.339-74.

[222] T = number of years.

[223] Bold letters indicate matrices.

[224] There is always one dummy variable less than the number of observations. Otherwise a model with our specifications would suffer from perfect collinearity.

[225] In practice, the large number of dummy variables can be avoided by expressing the regression equation as deviations from country means. This setup accounts for country fixed effects.

makes the random effects model more desirable for datasets with a limited number of observations.

Since one setup (the FE design) uses OLS regression techniques, violations of the classical assumptions are analyzed. Particular firm boundaries might change easier once they have changed for the first time, i.e. changes in firm boundaries might suffer from positive serial correlation. TUCKER/WILDER (1977) argue that it is easier for slightly integrated industries to increase their vertical integration than for more integrated ones, i.e. assuming negative serial correlation. Hence, autocorrelation would depend on the level of integration already reached in a particular country. I use country dummies to account for these country-level fixed effects. Cross-sectional data is often suspicious of heteroskedasticity, i.e. a violation of the OLS assumption of constant error variance. This is especially true for great variations in the size of the cross-sectional units.[226] A viable method of testing the model for heteroskedasticiy is to investigate plots of residuals.[227] They show no systematic pattern and hence no signs of heteroskedasticiy.

Correlation among the independent variables might be an issue. This would lead to multicollinearity. Perfect multicollinearity would violate the assumption of the classical OLS model that no explanatory variable is a perfect linear function of any other explanatory variable(s). To avoid collinearity, I will test different model specifications to avoid the joint inclusion of correlated variables.[228]

3.5.3   Results and Discussion

I estimate several versions of the model using both, fixed and random effects. The fact that significance levels and parameter magnitudes change in the FE model is not unexpected because the results obtained from different statistical models are driven by different assumptions about the unobservable heterogeneity. The data contains only a limited number of countries and therefore covers not the entire population of countries. In this situation, the selected group of countries – although they are pretty homogeneous – covers only a random sample from

---

[226] See STUDEMUND (1997), p. 99.

[227] See JOBSON (1992a), p. 169.

[228] The joint inclusion of correlated variables in a regression would lead to individually low significance scores would be low although the overall explanatory power of the complete regression equation is high. Different model specifications are used to avoid this problem.

the entire world population of countries which makes the RE setup more preferable.[229] The Hausman test favors the FE setup. However, the random specification can be rejected on a 5% level but not the 1% level for in regression (1). Hence, I report both, RE and FE model. The results are given in the following table.

Table 5: Test Results (Manufacturing)

Variables	(1)	(2)	(3)	(4)	(5)
SA_BY_AS	2.808581	-36.5443	1.839979	3.078625	2.08154
	(0.39)	(-1.86)	(0.50)	(0.91)	(0.71)
ICTI	-0.01488	-0.042	-0.04866	-0.041	-0.04245
	(-0.38)	(-0.95)	(-3.05)***	(-2.62)**	(-2.65)**
ICTPPC	-1.34568	-0.01718	1.084474	-0.60243	-0.87033
	(-0.74)	(-0.72)	(1.08)	(-0.51)	(-0.81)
ICTTPC	0.001816	0.000319	0.047991	0.044	0.041011
	(0.05)	(0.85)	(1.6)	(1.49)	(1.42)
LNINF	-0.10025	0.363514	-0.49662	-0.65209	-0.65794
	(-0.10)	(0.33)	(-0.88)	(-1.23)	(-1.26)
EXPGDP	3.821231	0.299958	7.03600	3.480154	3.274273
	(0.54)	(0.03)	(1.56)	(0.56)	(0.53
POLCON	-1.39157	-507.578	-5.76436	-4.05382	-3.4536
	(-0.35)	(-1.22)	(-2.63)**	(-1.88)*	(-1.82)
AS	-0.0009	0.000043	-0.00357	-0.00147	
	(-0.21)	(0.01)	(-1.49)	(-0.60)	
ATA	0.003437	0.005513	0.005057	0.003249	0.001961
	(0.78)	(1.15)	(2.23)**	(1.38)	(2.01)*
GDP	-0.00092	0.008721	-0.00208	-0.00059	-0.00071
	(-0.26)	(1.46)	(-1.04)	(-0.22)	(-0.27)
GDP_PC	-151.317	-438.939	92.58121	60.69128	75.08828
	(-0.77)	(-1.81)*	(1.04)	(0.51)	(0.65)
TAS_EMP	-0.21334	-0.062	0.293634	1.51518	1.609851
	(-0.33)	(-0.05)	(0.96)	(3.17)***	(3.61)***
LN_ANOE	1.948845	2.909027	0.26788	0.70191	0.590553
	(1.12)	(1.42)*	(0.28)	(0.66)	(0.57)
R_D	-2.67157		1.574579		
	(-0.39)		(0.6974)		
HIGH_CON	-0.43568		-2.47079		
	(-0.08)		(-0.93)		
RDSAAV	70.14695		21.39994	18.28056	19.92634
	(0.60)		(0.4)	(0.35)	(0.38)
Adjusted R2	0.1032	0.761	0.4704	0.9831	0.9828
NT	98	98	56	56	56
Model	RE	FE	RE	FE	FE

Figure in parentheses are t statistics (two-tailed tests). *, **, and *** denote significance at the 10%, 5%, and 1% levels respectively. FE model: country dummies are not reported for brevity.

---

[229] HSIAO (1986), p.43.

Due to high partial correlation of Internet hosts and Internet users per capita[230], I use only one measure of Internet penetration. For the full time period (1991 to 1997), the influence of Internet penetration on vertical integration is negative but insignificant. Both empirical setups show no significance in the ICT variable as seen in model (1) and (2). This might be related to the fact that the changes of the ICT environment affects the business architecture of firms in the latter half of the chosen time period. The cluster analysis performed earlier indicated that variation in the degree of ICT penetration is higher towards the end of the analyzed period: the cluster of country-years with high Internet penetration mainly contains years from the end of the observed period. Therefore, a regression is performed without the early country-years 1991 to 1993 in model (3) to (5).[231] Indeed, for the last four years of the analyzed time period (1994 to 1997) Internet penetration shows a significant negative impact on vertical integration on a 1% (RE) or 5% (FE) confidence level. The communication technology variables remain non-significant.[232]

Most control variables show the anticipated results. Capital intensity measured as total assets per employee (TAS_EMP) is significantly driving vertical integration. This is an expected result. Since (physical) asset specificity is usually a reason for asset specificity (an important determinant of vertical integration) the high significance is also anticipated.

Interestingly, political regimes with high POLCON scores tend to have slimmer firms. This might be related to the fact that vertical contracting is easier in politically stable environments making vertical integration unnecessary. This is not contradictory to the TCE-based explanation that slimmer firms need a sound institutional environment. Even though developed financial markets can foster (horizontal) growth, vertical growth can be replaced by down- or upstream outsourcing only when the institutional environment allows firms to legally control and enforce this contracting out. The explanation that firm growth is easier when firms find themselves in good institutional environment is consistent. The results only show that outsourcing up- and downstream might be facilitated in sound institutional environments. The other control variables turn out to be not significant because most of the

---

[230] Pearson's correlation coefficient is 0.54, significant on a 1% confidence level.
[231] I dropped one firm size measures (AS) from the regression to avoid multicollinearity and left the employee measure in model (5). Partial correlations among AS and AT are higher than between the employee measure and AS and/or AT. Except for showing a slight positive impact of firm size on vertical integration this did not induce any major changes to the model. Dropping both firm size measures only reduced some overall significance.

variance not explained by ICT is absorbed from the country dummies. Model versions with time lags did not yield any new results. A separate analysis of the Scandinavian countries revealed that vertical integration has been lower in the Scandinavian high ICT penetration group compared to the Scandinavian low ICT penetration group. In addition, omitting the Scandinavian countries from the sample reduced overall significance and significance of the ICT variables. Hence, a Scandinavia effect (i.e. generally lower vertical integration in Scandinavia drives the vertical integration-ICT relationship) is unlikely. The drop in significance without the Scandinavian countries necessitates further inquiry to verify that the identified relationship is not driven by a few not ICT-related outliers.[233]

Taking into account the empirical results the interpretation of ICT induced outsourcing can not be rejected. However, it is important to note that this effect is only measurable in the mid and late 1990s. This result is in accordance with both hypotheses stated above: firm boundaries are affected by ICT variance in terms of both, variance induced by increasing ICT penetration over time (H2) and variance in form of different levels of ICT development across countries (H1).

3.6 Conclusion

Manufacturing firm boundaries are contracting. The empirical examination of manufacturing firm boundaries provide evidence of a trend towards slimmer firm architectures that is driven partly by ICT. However, the results have to be interpreted with caution. Although firms appear to become slimmer as a result of advances in ICT on aggregate, there might be different degrees of suitability for outsourcing. These depend e.g. upon product life cycles that are not measured here because of the aggregated level of analysis.[234] Due to the research design, firm specific effects are neglected in order to gain results at the aggregate level.

Another limitation is that ICT is only one of a number of dimensions in the business environment that shape firm boundaries. As illustrated with the inclusion of a political

---

[232] An explanation might be that the Internet is a more disruptive technology than new telecommunication devices. At least, firm boundaries are solely affected by the former type of ICT and not the latter type.
[233] I checked the microdata for the Scandinavian firms in the sample and omitted outliers. The aggregated countries values for vertical integration without outliers changed only slightly and induced no change in the overall model significance.
[234] Usually, a dominant design or standardized form of a product component exists once the product has reached the maturity stage of the product life cycle. See UTTERBACK/SUÁREZ (1993) for further reference.

variable in my regression I argue that the political environment plays a role in shaping firm boundaries that is at least of equal importance. In addition, it is noteworthy to state that ICT has different faces. The whole variety of ICTs can not be fully reflected in the analysis even though I used several different ICT variables. There might be undetected differences in the organizational effects of different ICTs. My defense is that I focused on the most visible and presumably most disruptive technology, the Internet.

Despite these limitations, I demonstrated that ICT matters. I further identified the transaction environment as an important determinant of the organizational design of firms. The institutional environment is crucial for the morphology of firms that operate in a particular country at a particular time. TCE claims that the morphology of a firm is a function of the efficiency differential between hierarchy- and marked-based transaction governance forms. I provide (tentative) evidence that suggest shrinking firm boundaries in the manufacturing sector. This result is in line with the findings from casual empiricism at the begin of the analysis: by spinning of their supply divisions, GM and Ford can be seen as paradigmatic outsourcing examples. This is also comprehensible by taking the theoretical framework into consideration: firms adapt to the new ICT environment by drawing new firm boundaries. The new firm boundaries are more efficient in the new ICT environment. Ill-defined firm boundaries would represent a competitive disadvantage for firms. Therefore, firms aim to give themselves the appropriate organizational design that fits the new ICT environment.

In order to fully understand the mechanics of ICT-induced shifts in firm boundaries industry effects have to be taken into account. This poses the question if the results from the manufacturing sector in this chapter hold for other industries. The next chapter will leave the scope of the manufacturing sector as the subject of analysis and focus on media firms. The reason for this choice is that media firms deal with products that are affected by ICT in a different way than manufacturing firms. I will show in how far ICT-effects are different in this particular industry and finally rationalize the differences between the two industries using TCE.

4. Changing Firm Boundaries in the Media Sector

The trend in the manufacturing industries is pointing towards outsourcing and slimmer firms. One crucial determinant of this disintegration process has been innovation in ICTs. In other industries, the impact of ICT on firm boundaries is not necessarily the same. An evident example is the global media industry. Change in firm boundaries, i.e. merger & acquisitions (M&A) policies in the media sector, differs from the processes observed in the manufacturing sector. In the recent past, the entertainment and media industry has shown some structural changes that led to the formation of vertically integrated media groups. Firm boundaries are characterized by increasing vertical integration observable as vertical M&A activity. Evidence can be found in the literature that there is indeed a strong tendency for firms in the media industries to integrate vertically.[235] This chapter develops the interpretation that the central reason for the insourcing tendency in the media sector is the difference in product characteristics between the media and the manufacturing sector:[236] ICT facilitates inter-firm transactions with typical manufacturing products. In contrast, ICT subverts the appropriation of rents generated by selling intangible media products.

In order to elucidate the impact of new ICTs on media firm boundaries I analyze in particular the global market for recorded music. I look at the current organizational shape of global media firms and provide case examples for increasing backward and forward integration. In order to understand the observed structures and integration moves, I examine their efficiency in an eclectic theoretical framework. The result of the theoretical analysis is that vertically integrated media firms can be seen as hierarchical constructions to protect IPRs that are threatened by copyright piracy. This chapter shows that by expanding in a vertical direction, media firms aim to protect the rent stream they generate by selling IPRs that is threatened by ICT-enabled copyright piracy.

---

[235] See GARDINI (2002).
[236] The peculiarities of media products and their distinct characteristics in comparison to typical manufacturing products are described in chapter 4.1.

As a second step, an empirical analysis is conducted to identify ICT-induced effects in the global media industry. As shown in chapter 4.2.2, the global media industry is an oligopolistic industry with few players that operate on an international level. The small number of firms in the industry does not lend itself to study the effect of ICT through vertical integration measures. Hence, it is reasonable to assume that a direct empirical analysis of organizational change is more difficult and less meaningful compared to the manufacturing sector, which is less oligopolistic. Nevertheless, the media world represents a fruitful subject of analysis to show that the impact of ICT can be the reverse in terms of firm boundary change vis-a-vis the manufacturing sector. As an appropriate indirect way to capture the impact of ICT on media firms empirically, I study the sales of recorded music in different countries. My empirical analysis supports the results derived in the eclectic theory part: ICT penetration in terms of PCs and Internet hosts shows a negative correlation with the sales of IPRs in the form of recorded music, i.e. ICT erodes the rent streams of media firms. Vertical integration can be seen as a protective move by media firms to regain control over the rent streams they generate from selling IPRs. However, appropriate international laws are able to protect these rent streams. My results suggest that recent international IPR protection treaties initiated by the World Intellectual Property Organization (WIPO) are capable of protecting the rent streams.[237]

4.1   Peculiarities of Media Products

The media industry– compared to other industries – has some peculiarities with regard to the product characteristics. Media products can be described best as information goods.[238] Typical information goods are for instance recorded music, news articles, digital images, or computer software.[239] Information goods are goods that involve large amounts of intellectual property rights (IPRs). The three main properties of information goods are that they

---

[237] Both, the theoretical survey and the empirical study should contribute to the understanding of media firm boundary change. The economic downturn in 2001 and 2002 had a negative effect on the media industry according to THE ECONOMIST (2002b). This downturn can give some clarity regarding the role of inefficiently drawn firm boundaries in the problematic situation of the media industry. In particular, I examine in how far ICT affected firm boundaries and thereby induced changes in the size of the efficient media firm boundary. A discrepancy between efficient and factual media firm boundaries would be an explanation for troubled media firms. TCE suggests that firms with differences between efficient and factual firm boundaries chose suboptimal governance modes for their transactions. This is ceteris paribus a competitive disadvantage compared to firms with optimally drawn firm boundaries.

[238] A good introduction to the economics of information goods is given by SHAPIRO/VARIAN (1999).

[239] See BAKOS (2001), p. 8.

(i)   are experience goods,

(ii)   show high returns to scale (high fixed costs of production but a low marginal costs of reproduction), and

(iii)   have certain public good characteristics.

The first characteristic (experience good) means that the value of goods can only be determined after its consumption, i.e. valuing information is only possible ex-post (when the information has already been released).[240] The second characteristic (economies of scale) is related to the media production process. In contrast to other sectors the production process is characterized by large "first copy costs" that lead to vast economies of scale. The production costs of an additional copy of a movie that is shown in a movie theatre compared to the initial production costs are negligible. The amount of economies of scale varies among different media products. For example, television production has more economies of scale than newspaper publishing.[241] The economies of scale induced by large proportion of IPRs in most media products are benefiting large firms that are able to exploit the positive returns to scale on a global basis.[242] This makes the media industry an attractive study object for international business research. The third characteristic means that the consumption process of media goods usually shows no rivalry. For example, a movie watcher does not reduce the utility of another movie watcher. The public good characteristics are analyzed in depth in chapter 4.3.3.

Another important peculiarity is the existence of network effects.[243] This applies primarily to television and radio networks but also to Internet services. A good example are television networks: consumers joining a particular television network increase the value of the network by extending its income base for advertisement. Adding a user to the network induces low costs but raises the utility of the network as a whole. The phenomenon of network effects is evaluated in the conclusion of chapter four regarding its power to induce organizational

---

[240] This property is explained in further detail by ARROW's information paradox, see ARROW (1962).

[241] For a survey of the cost structures of different media products regarding first copy costs and distribution costs see ALTMEPPEN (1996).

[242] Using IPRs twice does not lead to a deterioration of value while fixed assets generally loose value through usage.

[243] SHAPIRO/VARIAN (1999), p. 173-225 give a good survey of network effects in the media markets. The value of a network increases with the number of its users. Due to structural redundancy the utility of a network increases faster than the costs of adding a marginal user which leads to network externalities. These externalities can induce collective switching costs and thereby create standards that are often associated with market power.

change: the market power associated with network effects[244] in a downstream market combined with upstream market power (oligopolistic media industry) provides a rationale for vertical integration according to double marginalization theory.

The description of the peculiarities of media products shows that media products differ to a great extent from the typical products in the manufacturing sector. For example, car components and semi-finished mobile phones are neither experience goods nor do they resemble public goods. Hence, the effect of ICT on the manufacturing and the music market is not necessarily identical. The following paragraph gives an overview of the media industry and portrays the most important changes in firm boundaries that have occurred in this sector.

4.2 The Global Media Industry: A Survey

4.2.1 The Media Market

The media industry production process consists of content producers that own the IPRs of some creative act (e.g. a movie or music), i.e. the 'content'.[245] The content is sold via a vast variety of channels to end-consumers (CDs, movie theatres etc.). Contracts between so-called content providers on the one side and access providers, i.e. distributors, on the other side can be regarded as a vertical link between producers and distributors. The value chains in the different media market sectors differ slightly but follow the same 'content-access' logic.[246]

Using a broad definition, the size of the global media industry is estimated at approximately 200bn USD per year.[247] It is characterized by an oligopolistic market structure with seven major players competing in the global marketplace as depicted in the figure below.

---

[244] Network effects exist if the utility of using a good depends upon other consumers using the same good. See Economides (1996).

[245] See WIRTZ (2001), p. 27.

[246] For an overview of the different value chains in the different media market sectors (music, publishing, television etc.) see ZERDICK ET AL (2000), p. 52-60.

[247] See VOGEL (2001). This figure refers to the amount of total sales in the segments broadcasting (TV & radio), cable TV, filmed entertainment, gaming (casinos), publishing (books, magazines, newspapers), recorded music, theatrical exhibition, theme parks, and toys.

Figure 11: Major Media Groups

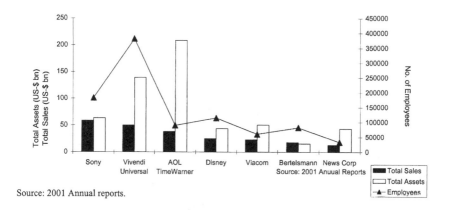

Source: 2001 Annual reports.

A number of mergers has increased the reach of the major media companies at the turn of the millennium.[248] In early 2000, the Internet firm AOL merged with Time Warner. In June 2000, French media and utilities group Vivendi merged with Seagram, owner of Universal Music, to form Vivendi Universal in December 2000. The USD 34bn merger combined the assets of Vivendi, Canal Plus[249], and Seagram (owner of Universal Studios and Universal Music).[250]

Recent mergers like Vivendi-Universal, and AOL-Time Warner can be interpreted as a vertical pattern caused by the formation of media firms that are integrated backward into content production and forward into new distribution channels like the Internet seem to prove that.[251] This makes us hypothesize that Time Warner (content) merging with AOL (access), and Vivendi (access) merging with Universal (content) can be seen as indicators for a tendency towards increasing vertical integration.

By looking at the organizational structure of the world's major media firms it becomes obvious that the existing industry structure is already characterized by vertical integration. By 2002, most of the seven big global media conglomerates had operations in the following sectors: Internet portals, broadcast television, cable television, telecommunication, film

---

[248] The integration process gained momentum in the mid 1990 with the repeal of the financial and syndication rules that allowed movie studios to own television channels, see WALKER/FERGUSON (1998).

[249] Canal Plus is Vivendi's pay-TV affiliate.

[250] The two mergers are described in THE ECONOMIST (2001c).

[251] Interestingly, Yahoo! Inc. installed a poison pill in February 2001 and can be interpreted as a defensive measure to avoid a potential hostile takeover by content producers like Viacom or Disney.

production, television production, music, publishing, theme parks, and radio. Their respective portfolio of operations is systematized in the table below.

Table 6: Operations of Global Media Conglomerates

	Internet Portal	Broadcast TV	Cable TV	Telecoms	Production		Music	Publishing	Theme Parks	Radio
					Film	TV				
Sony					✓	✓	✓			
Vivendi Universal	✓		✓	✓	✓	✓	✓	✓	✓	
Disney		✓	✓		✓	✓		✓	✓	✓
Bertelsmann		✓				✓	✓	✓		✓
AOL-Time Warner	✓	✓	✓		✓	✓	✓	✓		✓
News Corporation		✓	✓		✓	✓		✓		
Viacom		✓	✓		✓	✓		✓		✓

Source: THE ECONOMIST (2002a).

Many of the operations performed by global media firms can be assigned to subsequent stages of production in order to analyze the paradigmatic value-chain of media firms. The logic of content and access developed earlier can be used to assign the various operations to different production stages. A piece of content is produced (for example a movie is shot), aggregated (packed in a movie theater release, a DVD, and a CD with the soundtrack), and later distributed (shown in movie theaters, sold as CD and DVD in record stores). It becomes obvious that the operations follow a vertical logic as depicted in the following figure.

Figure 12: Vertical Reach of Global Media Conglomerates

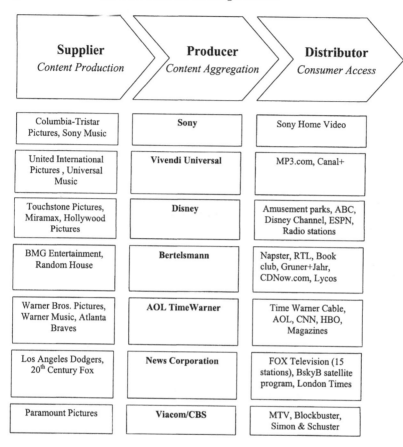

Source: annual reports, various years.

An important sector in the global media industry in the segment for recorded music. It is also a market where the impact of ICT is considered to be strong. Consequently, it constitutes an appropriate example to study organizational transformation that is induced by ICT.

4.2.2 The Music Market

The five major players in the music market are Universal Music commanding a market share of 23%, Sony Music [15%], EMI [14%], Warner Music [13%], and Bertelsmann Music

Group (BMG) [12%].[252] The worldwide market for recorded music comprised USD 33.7bn in 2001 but showed a decline recently. The global music market fell 5% in value and 6.5% in sales.[253] Innovations in ICT like music sharing over the Internet are accused of harming the music industry notably. Demand for music is supposed to remain strong but the availability of free music via digital mass copying is blamed to depress sales figures.[254] The sales decrease raises questions regarding the reasons for this drop and the role of ICT as a potential cause of it. I will examine this question in chapter 4.4.3 empirically.

The impact of ICT on music firm boundaries is not entirely new. Historically, music reproduction has been invented by Thomas A. Edison in 1877 through the development of the phonograph and later been improved by A. Graham Bell.[255] The phonograph was the result of two other inventions, the telegraph and the telephone. In 1890, Emile Berliner developed the Grammophon that was later brought to the market by the Victor Taking Machine Company.[256] Reproduction technology has evolved over time. After World War II, Vinyl was introduced as the principal storage medium for music. HiFi-Stereo recording followed in the 1960s and the compact disc (CD) in 1983.

Recently, low cost and low effort private duplication of music tracks became feasible. In the mid 1990s, scientists at the Fraunhofer Institute for Integrated Circuits (IIS-A) developed the audio coding algorithm MPEG Layer-3 (MP3). It allows to compress music files to 1/10 to 1/12 of its size[257] which makes them suitable for Internet-based exchange in so-called peer-to-peer (P2P) networks like Napster. Napster uses a central server to administer to locations of music files that are swapped via the Internet. Other P2P systems do not use a central server but direct connections between owners/possessors of MP3 files. The latter system is hard to control because its structure is decentralized and does not require a legal entity (e.g. a firm) to run it. The "napsterization" process might also happen to other media products like movies because of very similar product features.

---

[252] LEHMAN BROTHERS (2001), p. 18.
[253] Figures according to the International Federation of the Phonographic Industry (IFPI), the organization representing the recording industry worldwide.
[254] See IFPI (2001), p. 3 and IFPI (2002a), p. 3.
[255] See VOGEL (2001), p. 128.
[256] See WIRTZ (2001), p. 347.
[257] See WIRTZ (2001), p. 348.

On October 31, 2000, Napster, Inc. and Bertelsmann AG have formed an alliance in an attempt to further develop the musicfile-swapping software maker's products and services (Napster II). According to the terms of the deal, Bertelsmann assisted in Napster's development of a secure, membership-based distribution service for music files over the Internet via providing a loan of USD 50m. In May 2001, Vivendi Universal made a similar move by acquiring online music distribution company MP3.com for USD 372m. By mid 2002, Napster has been banned from providing music over the Internet for free by successful copyright infringement lawsuits.[258] As a result, all global music firms have offered subscription-based online music services called Pressplay (formerly known as "Duet") (Sony, Vivendi) and MusicNet (AOL-Time Warner, BMG).[259] The entirety of these mergers and alliances show the ambition of media firms to establish secure online distribution arms.

All the transactions just described have a common organizational rationale: media firms aim to control the online distribution process. The creation of online subscription platforms is a de facto downstream vertical integration strategy. Record companies integrate downstream into online distribution channels. Optimistic market research exists that projects online distribution to grow to a USD 1.6bn market in 2006, with USD 1bn coming from subscriptions.[260] The acceptance for digital consumption forms of music is growing. Online music sites reached 100m US customers by October 2001 as presented in the following figure:

Figure 13: Usage of Online Music Sites (US only)

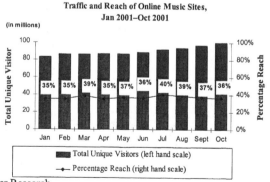

Source: Jupiter Research

[258] In mid 2000, the Recording Industry Association of America (RIAA) successfully sued the online music file exchange provider Napster for copyright infringements.
[259] Subscription-based services charge a fixed fee per period of time that is independent from transaction frequency.
[260] See JUPITER RESEARCH (2001), p.1.

In the following paragraphs, I will try to give theoretical motivations for the observed conduct of media firms with a focus on the music industry. This will shed some light on the motivation of the media industry's 'move-to-the-hierarchy' and the role of record companies as integral parts of media conglomerates. The increasing importance of ICT will be examined in its role as a determinant of the pattern we observe. Thereby the efficiency of the existing firm boundaries and firm boundary changes can be evaluated. By determining the efficiency of recently drawn firm boundaries the viability of these structures in the time of economic downturns can be assessed. This might contribute to enhance our understanding of reverse integration tendencies.

4.3   Theories of Media Firm Boundary Change

In order to give an adequate assessment of the change in firm boundaries in the media sector I use an eclectic approach. Therefore, I employ three theoretical rationales, i.e. (i) an industrial organization (IO) framework, (ii) Incomplete Contract Theory, and (iii) Public Good Theory. This proceeding can be criticized for being eclectic because of an inconsistent theoretical framework. I argue that the novelty of the phenomenon justifies the application of three different theories because the lessons learned from each theory are slightly different but all meaningful.[261] All theories that I apply add another facet to our understanding of ICT impact on organizational change.[262] There are two principal phenomena to be motivated in the eclectic theoretical framework: In chapter 4.3, I will first rationalize the high degree of vertical integration that is observable in the media sector and then evaluate the role of record companies to be a part of vertically integrated media firms in the light of the theory from three different theoretical angles.

4.3.1   Safeguarding Specific Assets

GARDINI (2002) provides a TCE-based motivation for the circumstance that motion picture studios own television networks. As described in earlier chapters the unit of analysis in TCE is the transaction. There are two principal transactions between movie studios and television stations:[263] (i) movie studios licensing the rights of film libraries to television broadcasters,

---

[261] Hence, the characteristics of media products are mentioned not only in the introductory part of chapter four, but also in the different subchapters of chapter four that form the eclectic approach.
[262] The objective of the eclectic approach is that every theory should shed light on another facet of the truth.
[263] See GARDINI (2002), p.10.

and (ii) movie studios producing television series and selling the rights to the television broadcasters.

According to WILLIAMSON (1975, 1985) transactions differ in terms of their transaction dimensions frequency, uncertainty, and asset specificity that lead to quasi rents.[264] Usually, transactions of type (i) do not require hierarchical governance because frequency, uncertainty, and asset specificity is low. The same movie is licensed only once or at least in long intervals, its value is known from the appearance in the theatrical market, and specific investments to promote the movie on TV are relatively low.

The transactions in which movie studios sell a television series to a television broadcaster (type (ii)) have a different structure. After the first season is sold and broadcast, the television station has usually invested heavily in promoting the series. It thereby created quasi-rents because the promotion investments are idiosyncratic. Market governance would lead to inefficient haggling over these quasi-rents between the producer and the broadcaster making vertical integration the most efficient solution in this context.

This would provide a reasonable theoretical rationale for the existing vertical links like Fox Television-20th Century Fox, ABC-Disney or Universal Studios-Canal Plus.

The case is different regarding the integration of online music retailers. To assess if the vertical links between global media conglomerates and online music retailers are justified, the transactions over this interface have to be examined. The obvious rationale is to distribute existing music content via the Internet.

Transactions in which record labels sell music to retailers traditionally did not require any specific investments. As long as the music that consists of IPRs is physically attached to a storage medium (a CD) the transaction can be executed via the market. Consumers could not separate the IPRs from the storage medium, i.e. the CD or the record, because of insufficient

---

[264] The concept of quasi-rents stems from KLEIN ET AL (1978) and has a precursor in A. Marshall's "composite quasi-rents", see MARSHALL (1952).

copying technology. As long as copying technology was inefficient[265] and copyright law could be enforced technically[266] the product was tangible or at least "tangiblized".

Progress in ICT made copying technology cheaper and more efficient which allowed consumer to separate the IPRs from the legally acquired music storage medium. ICT made it feasible for consumers to create an identical low-cost copied CD or swap the compressed music recording via the Internet, i.e. "reintangiblize" the IPRs. As we know from empirical TCE research[267], intangible assets are often the source of asset specificity and hence exchanged best via hierarchical interfaces and not via market interfaces. Additionally, music firms invest heavily in the production and marketing of their artists. These investments are usually bound to a particular artist and thereby highly specific. Given that music firms cannot recoup these investments by selling CDs these investments are lost. According to TCE logic hierarchical governance modes are able to govern transactions that would not take place in an open market. Within a hierarchy that safeguards these specific assets production and distribution can be controlled. By owning online music retailers record companies expect to gain control over the distribution process. If record companies manage to restrict technically the unrestricted usage of a music file that is distributed online[268], the result resembles a transaction in which the consumer would have to buy the regular CD. Hierarchies are used by media firms intending to increase control over the music distribution process.[269]

In the case of music, TCE helps to understand the move towards more hierarchical governance structures: the price mechanism is inferior to govern the exchange process of intangible goods compared to the hierarchy. Ceteris paribus, ICT changes the characteristics of media products by turning tangible goods (e.g. CDs) into intangible goods (digital music files).[270] This affects the optimal governance mode and leads to the emergence of more and more hierarchical forms of exchange.

---

[265] Before CD burners allowed to create digital clones copies like music tapes for private usage did not separate the IPRs from the storage medium in an adequate way.
[266] Enforcing copyrights when compressed music files can be exchanged via the Internet can be considered to be non-trivial.
[267] See e.g. CAVES/BRADBURD (1988).
[268] E.g. by technically limiting future copying acts.
[269] The possibility that legally acquired CD are copied using a CD burner and a PC is avoided by using watermarks or other technical IPR protection mechanisms.
[270] This applies in analogy to a number of other products with a high degree of IPRs. By transforming scientific journal articles from their paper-based version into a digital form they loose their tangible character.

4.3.2 Avoiding Double Marginalization

Forward and backward integration by firms in general can be explained in an IO framework with the double marginalization rationale as developed by SPENGLER (1950).[271] This rationale can be applied to the media sector by analyzing the integration decision between the production stages of integrated media firms on the one side and online music retailers and integrated media groups on the other side. In a market structure with two imperfect markets in a vertical order, double marginalization can occur. It is an efficient organizational response to internalize vertical externalities. I will present a simple version of the problem that may elucidate the integration incentives here.

An upstream (content) producer P sells his product at price w (wholesale price) to the downstream distributor D (access provider). D charges price p (retail price) for the good in a imperfectly competitive market with demand x=1-p.

In the non-integration case, the producer pursues a monopolistic pricing strategy in stage one of the game followed by stage two in which the distributor adds another monopolistic mark-up to the price. The game can be solved using backwards induction starting with the distributor and a given w. The distributor makes the following profit

$$\pi_D = (1-p)(p-w)$$

first order condition (FOC):

$$\frac{\partial \pi_D}{\partial p} = 1\text{-}2p\text{+}w \overset{!}{=} 0$$

$$\Rightarrow p^* = \frac{1+w}{2} \text{ such that equilibrium demand is } x^* = \frac{1-w}{2}.$$

The producer now maximizes profit for quantity x^*

$$\pi_P = \frac{1-w}{2} w$$

[271] For a good survey looking at the contributions from Industrial Organization Theory to vertical integration research, see TIROLE (1992), p. 169-208.

FOC:

$$\frac{\partial \pi_P}{\partial p} = \frac{1}{2}(1-2w)$$

$\Rightarrow$ w* = $\frac{1}{2}$ which gives us x* = $\frac{1}{4}$ and p* = $\frac{3}{4}$

It is easy to show that vertical integration would lead to

$$x^* = w^* = p^* = \frac{1}{2}$$

which is pareto-superior in terms of output and price to the non-integration case with

$$x^* = \frac{1}{4}, w^* = \frac{1}{2} \text{ and } p^* = \frac{3}{4}.$$

The equations show that – assumed there is a monopolistic upstream market (input market) – downstream purchasers will have to pay the monopoly mark-up. If the downstream market is also monopolistic the final price will have two mark-ups. Hence the price is higher ($\frac{3}{4} > \frac{1}{2}$) and the quantity is lower ($\frac{1}{4} < \frac{1}{2}$) in the non-integration situation compared to the integrated solution. The same applies with reduced mark-ups if both markets are at least oligopolistic, i.e. market power exists. The overall outcome can now be improved in terms of pooled-profits/welfare[272] via vertical integration.

The market structure just described is often understood as a form of vertical externality, i.e. the retailer does not take into account the manufacturer's marginal profit, as shown by TIROLE (1992, p. 174). Vertical integration leads to an internalization of this externality.

Is this a convincing theoretical motivation for the description of the industry structure in the media sector? If double marginalization is a valid explanation for the vertical phenomenon in the media sector I would expect market imperfections up- and downstream. For theoretical reasons this seems to be the case for traditional media, i.e. the existence of integrated media conglomerates, but not necessarily for downstream integration into online distribution.

The simplified music production process roughly comprises four stages.[273] It starts with the production of creative content by an artist who presents his work to a record company. When the quality screening mechanism – in form of the artist and repertoire (A&R) department – is

---

[272] The vertical integration outcome can be evaluated in terms of pareto-superiority (welfare implication).

passed the record company acquires the intellectual property rights (IPRs) from the artist and produces a music album.[274] The rights to the thereby created master tape are usually owned by a music publishing company.[275] The master tapes then enter the duplication process that is governed by licensing agreements with the music publishing house. The range of possible licensing agreements increases within the new media group architectures. The music IPRs can be licensed for new and related media products like video games, or DVDs. In the subsequent stage, the recording sold using the marketing techniques of the record company to different types of users. Users include private consumers and broadcasting entities like radio and music television. The IPR owner receives the revenues from sound storage media sales (first use, distribution) and broadcasting royalties from a collecting society[276] (second use, transmission). The following figure shows the traditional music value chain.

Figure 14: Music Value Chain (Past)

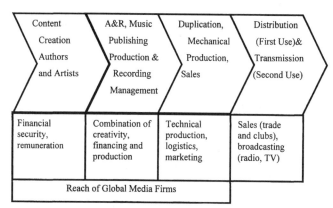

Source: ZERDICK ET AL (2000), p. 54.

With the emergence of new forms of ICT the value chain has been extended. Private duplication via CD copying and music sharing over the Internet has added a stage of cheap and high-quality private duplication.

---

[273] See WIRTZ (2001), p. 341.

[274] IPRs in the music industry can be separated into two main categories. There are the rights to the composition (the sheets). Typically, they are owned by the publishing company. The other category includes the performance and duplication rights, see VOGEL (2001), p. 138.

[275] The music publishing companies are typically part of an integrated media group, e.g. Sony/ATV Music Publishing, EMI Music Publishing, Universal MCA Publishing, Warner/Chappel Music, BMG-UFA.

[276] Important collecting societies are GEMA (Gesellschaft für musikalische Aufführungs- und mechanische Vervielfältigungsrechte) in Germany, and BMI (Broadcast Music Inc.) in the US.

Figure 15: Music Value Chain (Present, without IPR Protection)

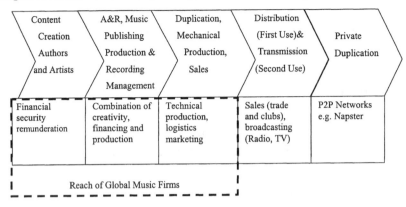

Source: own figure based on ZERDICK ET AL (2000), p. 54.

As mentioned before, music companies have started to acquire online music retailers and thereby increased their degree of vertical integration as shown in the following picture.

Figure 16: Music Value Chain (Present, with IPR Protection)

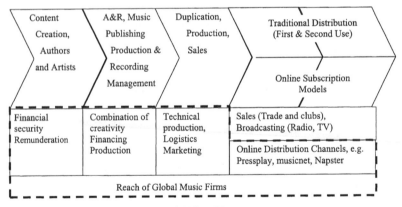

Source: own figure based on ZERDICK ET AL (2000), p. 54.

By applying the double marginalization rationale this firm boundary change can be evaluated theoretically. Music production can be defined as the upstream market and online music retailing can be defined as the downstream market. To justify vertical integration processes between music producers and online music retailers market power in both stages is required.

The market structure in the upstream industry (music production) can be seen as an indicator for imperfect competition in this field. The existence of only a handful of global media firms is not contradictory to the interpretation that the global music market is oligopolistic.[277] The music value chain can help to understand where these imperfections are located. Publishers and A&R managers[278] are usually part of the big music companies. This structure might stem from large marketing costs associated with selling sufficient output to meet minimum efficient scale. The intangibility of the content might be another issue that leads to entities large enough to exploit the significant economies of scale in the supply structure of the market. The intangibility is also a driver of cross-selling economies. The rights to a particular music track can be sold e.g. as an album CD and as part of a movie soundtrack. Selling the same IPRs through different channels within an integrated media group exploits vast economies of scale.[279]

In the downstream segment (online music retailing), the case is less clear. New (online) distribution firms gain market power and create switching costs through the bundling of goods and services (dynamically updating customized content, i.e. presenting music products online) and thereby add value to the inputs purchased from the content provider. Market power from a strong brand and high customer loyalty that would lead to market imperfections is not evident.[280] This was expected to be the case with Napster but the emergence of a vast variety of alternative music download services in the meantime suggests that this can be doubted.

Commercial P2P services charging for their usage would have strong network externalities in consumption because the value/utility of the P2P-network depends upon the number of users. A linearly increasing number of users implies an overproportional increase of the number of

---

[277] For example, 70% of all spending for US-screenwriting is done by the six big media conglomerates, see THE ECONOMIST (2002a), and 75% of recorded music sales are supplied by the five big record labels, see LEHMAN BROTHERS (2001). This domination of a few global players allows an interpretation of the music market as an oligopolistic market.

[278] See INTERNATIONAL DATA CORPORATION (2000): A&R be understood as a talent screening mechanism. There are approximately 20,000 albums released each year of which 90 percent sell only few (less than 10,000) copies.

[279] The process might be limited by artistic and creative dilution. WIRTZ (2001) argues that small record companies often show higher degrees of creativity. This might stem from the fact that they can pursue less established artistic strategies.

[280] In the zenith of Napster's existence the subscription service had 13.6m users, but lost its user base quickly to other services once the functionality had been reduced, see THE ECONOMIST (2002c).

connections between these users.[281] This is certainly based on market entry assumptions. If market entry barriers are high the market is not contestable[282] and hence more monopolistic. The current music online retailer MusicNet (by EMI, Bertelsmann, and the software firm Real Networks) and Pressplay (by Sony Music and Universal/Vivendi)[283] have failed to attract a critical mass of users in order to create network externalities.[284] Hence, double marginalization in the music market might not be the case because of missing market power in the downstream segment. This makes integration of online music retailers by record companies (and ultimately by their parent media companies) an inefficient firm boundary change. Strictly, double marginalization does not predict vertical integration activity but provides a theoretical rationale to show the efficiency of integration versus market-based transactions.

The integration process in the media industry as a whole makes sense given that both, content production and media retail markets are loci of imperfect competition. For example, the AOL-Time Warner merger is supposed to be characterized by a vertical integration rationale.[285] The merger objective has been to distribute the Time Warner 'Content' through AOL's Internet customers.[286]

Double marginalization is an explanation for a merger of two sequential monopolies. This is not necessarily the case in all segments of the media market. The reason is that existence of a monopoly owned by AOL in the market for Internet services (downstream market) can be doubted. Once Internet access becomes a commodity AOL lacks market power in the Internet

---

[281] For bilateral connections in a network the utility increases approximately with the square of the number of users n, i.e. n(n-1). See ECONOMIDES (1996).

[282] The theory of contestable markets by BAUMOL ET AL (1982) says that markets with a small number of competitors may not lead to monopoly pricing if market entry and exit barriers are moderate.

[283] This describes the structure in early 2002.

[284] Markets with network effects have distinct characteristics. According to KATZ/SHAPIRO (1994) firms gain market power by attracting a critical mass of users for their products that are distributed over a network: future users refrain from using other products for incompatibility reasons. They use the term 'excess inertia' to describe the effect that firms achieve market power by gaining a critical mass of users for their products distributed over a network.

[285] There are several other cases of vertical integration in the media sector, see ALBARRAN/DIMMICK (1996). These cases include Fox's (access) ownership of the 20th Century Fox movie library (content). Similarly, Disney Co. acquired Capital Cities/ABC and its 10 TV stations, 21 radio stations, and interest in several cable networks for USD 19 bn in 1996.

[286] This is largely equivalent to the idea of "cross-selling" a piece of creative work like music in different forms of media products.

end-consumer market to distribute the Time Warner content.[287] Today, consumers have a broad choice of Internet service providers and online services of which AOL only represents one possibility. Without this market power the assumptions of the double marginalization model are violated: the combination of AOL and Time Warner is not a merger of two sequential monopolies.

The double marginalization explanation for vertical integration relies on market power arguments. For the AOL-Time Warner merger, up- and downstream market power is not evident because Internet service provision is becoming a commodity. For the case of music distribution the conclusion is different. Upstream music markets can be seen as oligopolistic markets as noted in chapter 4.2.3. In the music market, the retail segment of online music distribution is crucial for existence of a double price mark-up. Double marginalization provides only a rationale for vertical integration if enough market power among end-consumers is achieved that justified a mark-up over the marginal cost price.

Chapter 4.3.2 demonstrated that IO Theory adds a market structure point of view to the analysis that is less central in other theories. Since IO Theory uses a more or less neoclassical set of assumptions, e.g. perfect rationality, it is indispensable to add other theories with less rigid assumptions. The explanation provided by IO Theory is mainly that certain media market structures lead to the creation of externalities that can be internalized using a hierarchy, i.e. a firm. The nature of this externality and the (ir-)rationality of the actors is neglected. These two points become clearer by applying the contract paradigm that takes into account imperfect rationality in the following chapter.

4.3.3   Overcoming Incomplete Contracts

Incomplete Contract Theory[288] can be used to provide a motivation for the vertical M&A patterns in the media industry. We know from TCE that a hold-up problem as a form of vertical externality arises when specific asset situations trigger ex-post opportunistic behavior in the form of appropriation of quasi-rents which leads to under-investment in specific assets

---

[287] MACKIE-MASON (2000) doubts that and emphasizes AOL TimeWarner's dominant position in the Internet end-consumer market.
[288] Seminal contributions to Incomplete Contract Theory are GROSSMAN/HART (1986), HART/HOLMSTROM (1987), HART/MOORE (1988).

in the first place.[289] Asset specificity is the consequence of investments in assets that have great differences in utility between their first-best and second-best use. Quasi-rents are residual control rights over an asset that can not be specified in a contract.

The incentives to appropriate these quasi-rents are given by opportunism. Incomplete Contract Theory introduced a contract view of the governance problem: transaction costs stem from information problems making contracts incomplete. These information problems accrue because of either lacking foresight or insufficient verifiability of actions. Imperfect foresight describes the fact that it is impossible and/or too costly to write down all possible contingencies in advance. Given that the future states of the world are observable they might not be verifiable to outsiders.[290] Hence, contracts are deemed to be incomplete. Asymmetries of information between contractors are not necessary assumption for incompleteness. It is sufficient to assume that information is not available to outsiders like courts and thus unverifiable.[291] What is the implication for business organization?

Efficient integration occurs when ex-post haggling over quasi-rents (i.e. residual non-contractible property rights) can be suppressed using a hierarchy (to align incentives). In Incomplete Contract Theory, non-integration leads to the hold-up result (i.e. under-investment occurs, transaction might be avoided) while integration in the form of buyer integration is – under certain conditions – superior in terms of Nash-bargained pooled profits compared to the non-integration case. This is true even though distortions remain and the first-best solution can not be achieved in the world of incomplete contracts. The mere non-contractibility of quasi-rents can lead to the avoidance of a transaction unless the market mechanism is replaced by a hierarchy.

A quantitative model of incomplete contracting is given in GROSSMAN/HART (1986). They explain the resulting degree of vertical integration using the risks of opportunistic behavior in the form of hold-ups as their method of argumentation to motivate the driving and limiting factors of a particular governance structure. WILLIAMSON (1996) considers their contribution,

---

[289] See KLEIN ET AL (1978).
[290] See HART (1987), p. 754.
[291] BROUSSEAU/FARES (2000) argue that there are differences between TCE (in the sense of WILLIAMSON) and Incomplete Contract Theory. The main difference is the set of assumptions. They note that Incomplete Contract Theory focuses on contractual choices subject to judicial verifiability constraints provided by the institutional

the Incomplete Contract Theory, to be a formalization of his insights. According to WILLIAMSON (1975, 1985) a party can protect its specific investment against a potential hold-up by merging with the opposite contracting party. In a supplier-producer relationship, the result is vertical integration. Theoretically, a completely specified contract in a market-based transaction could fulfill the same goal, but positive contractualization costs and bounded rationality make contracts necessarily incomplete.

The GROSSMAN/HART model[292] is a formalization of the hold-up problem that arises when specific asset situations trigger ex-post opportunistic behavior. Both parties have monopolistic power although there may be fierce competition before investments are sunk. Markets can not prevent exploitation through opportunistic behavior (hold-up) once their transaction is underway. Therefore, long-term contracts are made to divide the gains from their transaction. Due to transaction costs in the form of information problems contracts remain incomplete. The information problems are not caused by asymmetries of information between contractors but the struggle starts when the information is not available to outsiders like courts and hence unverifiable. According to GROSSMAN/HART vertical integration is a vehicle to avoid these hold-ups.

The principal result of the GROSSMAN/HART model can be summarized as follows: when contract specification is too costly it might be optimal for one party to purchase all rights except those specifically mentioned in the contract. The result of the purchase of the residual rights of control is vertical integration. GROSSMAN/HART develop the transaction cost theory one step further by comparing a contract that allocates all residual rights to one party with a contract allocating them to another. Before, the comparison has been made between a non-integrated relationship with incomplete contracts on the one side and integration with complete contracts (first-best solution) on the other.

GROSSMAN/HART dwell on their findings that integration shifts the incentives for opportunistic behavior to one party but does not remove these incentives. Integration in the form of buyer integration is – under certain conditions – superior compared to the non-

---

environment. In contrast, they consider TCE to be the joint generation of governance structures by individual actors and institutions (collective governance structures).

[292] GROSSMAN/HART (1986) as presented by TIROLE (1992), p. 31-33 and FURUBOTN/RICHTER (1989),p. 232-239.

integration case but distortions do not vanish and the first-best solution can not be achieved in the world of incomplete contracts.[293] Ownership is the second-best solution to protect one's investment.

This insight crucially depends on the following assumptions of the GROSSMAN/HART model: certain variables in the model can not be verified by outsiders, i.e. they are noncontractible. This unverifiability finally leads to underinvestment and allocational distortions.[294] However, the model shows an optimal second-best solution, i.e. vertical integration in an incomplete contracting environment.

A central weakness of the model is the fact that transaction costs are exogenous.[295] They are split into ex ante transaction costs (writing costs) and ex post transaction costs (non-verifiability of contracts). According to TIROLE (1994), the model has a certain inconsistency: the substantive rationality implied in the calculus of the transaction partners and the bounded rationality that is necessary to justify the ex ante transaction costs. Ex post transaction costs are based on the hypothesis that contracts contain non-verifiable information.

This type of information problem can be overcome by completing the incomplete contract with a revelation mechanism. MOORE (1992) criticizes that the revelation mechanism needs the assumption of (i) an unpaid judge, and (ii) a high, non-renegotiable default penalty. Apart from assumption (i) being doubtful, HART/HOLMSTRØM (1987) note that non-renegotiability does not comply with the assumption of opportunistic behavior. HART (1995) emphasizes the apparent incentives to renegotiate in situations with mutual benefits.

What is the relevance of Incomplete Contract Theory in the context of the media sector? I claim that Incomplete Contract Theory is a valuable framework to refer to in order to understand better why media firms vertically integrate. By applying this framework, two

---

[293] In a situation where parties have to agree in advance to decide upon trading with each other the transaction itself might be avoided. This is the case when both parties know that the other party will have the incentive to appropriate the quasi-rent even if oneself would abstain from it. The mere noncontractibility of quasi-rents can lead to the avoidance of a transaction.

[294] HART/MOORE (1988) tried to overcome the underinvestment problem by analyzing the optimal design for the revision game to be played once the unknown state of the world is realized. AGHION ET AL (1990, 1991) argue that the problem of unverifiability can be tackled by developing an optimal contractual renegotiation design (a kind of meta-contracting). This merely shifts the problem to another level.

[295] See BROUSSEAU/FARES(2000), p. 408.

crucial points in media sector analysis are crystallized: the product characteristics and the market structure.

In order to rationalize vertical media conglomerates as the result of incomplete contracting the product characteristics have to be analyzed. The product characteristics in the media sector are different from the products in other sectors, namely the manufacturing sector. The obvious difference is that music and movies are intangible products while products in the manufacturing industry (e.g. standardized semi-finished car parts) are typically tangible. This variance in product characteristics leads to a variance in the effect of ICT on the industry structure. A reasonable interpretation is that ICT seemed to have lowered transaction costs making outsourcing easier for manufacturing firms. The impact on the media market is different. My central argument is that ICT made contracts less complete for media product transactions between high-street CD merchants and CD buyers.

This argument can be substantiated with the following line of reasoning. Due to ICT, sellers of media products can specify less complete contracts for their transactions because copying of their intangible products is uncontrolled once the media product is sold to an end-consumer. Hence, the optimal industry structure (understood as supply chain governance) moves towards more vertical integration in the media industry. A possible and plausible interpretation is that ICT increased the incompleteness of contracts in the music value chain. Technologies like low-cost private duplication (CD burners) and high-quality private exchange networks (P2P networks) increased the incompleteness of the sales contract of a CD sold via traditional (high-street) distribution channels.[296] The result has been an enlargement of the set of future states of the world that can no longer be contracted for in the sales contract. Uncontrolled private duplication has not been a major issue without the existence of digital copying technology or high-quality file-swapping techniques (P2P technology). It has also been contained by the relatively poor quality of audio tapes made by owner of legally obtained pieces of recorded music.

---

[296] This becomes clearer if the discussion on private duplication is taken into account. Private copies of CDs have always been legal but used to have a poor quality and thereby did not harm the sales of legal high-quality CDs. Today, private, digital CD copies represent a threat because their quality is not different from the original CD.

This situation has changed fundamentally: consumer can distribute unprotected music files via P2P systems among themselves. If music companies sell music wholesale to distributors in form of record stores unauthorized further distribution by consumers cannot be avoided. Contracts on music sales are made in a legal and technological environment that can no longer guarantee their enforcement. Copyright law that governs the sales contract specifies that only a small number of legal duplications for private use can be made from the purchased music. This contractual provision cannot be enforced when consumers own CD burners and P2P technology that reduces the cost of reproduction plus the cost of distribution that helped to protect copyrights.[297] Hence, music firms have to internalize the sales process in order to control it. The acquisitions of online distribution channels by media firms (e.g. mp3.com by Vivendi and Napster by Bertelsmann) can be seen as attempts to gain control over the distribution process. By owning online music retailers record companies can or at least aim to oversee and control the sales process by implementing its own digital rights management systems (DRM systems)[298] or watermarks. Since the phenomenon of online distribution is rather young, it is too early to give a final evaluation of the success of this downstream integration strategy.

These IPR protection technologies allow the integrated music firms to channel the revenues from the retail market back to the IPR owner. In the case of non-integration the distribution cannot be controlled.

Without a protection mechanism for intellectual property rights, these increased contract enforcement costs can be regarded as ex-post transaction costs[299] or externalities that have been internalized by media companies integrating downstream in a 'move-to-the-hierarchy'. Even if ICT helped to decrease search costs (finding a particular music track online with P2P

---

[297] ICT led to the effect that the provision of copies of recorded music is no longer restricted to the retail outlet stage. Due to ICT private duplication is cheap and uncomplicated. Applying the Incomplete Contract Paradigm, this does not mean that AOL should own the consumer but internalize the duplication stage of the value chain back into the firm.

[298] SCHREIER ET AL (2000) defines DRM as „technology that protects content against unauthorized access, monitors the use of content, or enforces restrictions on what users can do with content." See appendix VI for further explication.

[299] Ex-post transaction costs include the cost of contract enforcement etc. In contrast, ex-ante transaction costs are e.g. search costs to find and identify the transaction partner, see WILLIAMSON (1985).

software is not very complicated) and thereby ex-ante transaction costs the increase of ex-post transaction costs is overcompensating this effect by increasing total transaction costs.[300]

Apart from the music market, Incomplete Contract Theory can provide a rationale for other media sectors, too. GARDINI (2002) argues that the sudden and unexpected success of a particular TV series can lead to hold-up situations. If a television channel acquires the IPRs for one season of a television series from a producer, the investments in the popularity of the series (i.e. advertising expenses) are sunk. The success of a TV program shown right after the success series profits from the audience generated before via the successful television series. Given that the series becomes a large success the upstream TV producer can increase his price for the IPRs of the season significantly. This can be interpreted as a hold-up of the downstream broadcaster to appropriate the quasi rents associated with the advertising revenues of the subsequent TV program. This has been the case for the successful television series 'Emergency Room' with Warner Brothers in the producer role and NBC as the distributor.[301] Hence, integration of TV producers and broadcaster make sense according to Incomplete Contract Theory. VOGEL (2001) found that both, equity-stakes of broadcasters in production firms increased and the number of own productions from broadcasters rose. This finding is compatible with Incomplete Contract Theory: producers aim to avoid hold-ups by broadcasters.

Incomplete Contract Theory can help to understand the impact of ICT on media industry organization using a contract paradigm. The writing of contracts in incomplete contracting environments is an inefficient governance mode for a transaction. The reason for this inefficiency is that the inclusion of all contingencies in the contract is impossible or at least too expensive. Integrated media firms can be interpreted as vehicles to overcome incomplete contracts by replacing the price mechanism between two stages of the value chain with hierarchical control.

In contrast to the results from double marginalization theory, downstream integration into online music retailers makes sense for music firms. Market imperfections are explained as increasing ex-post transaction costs that can be internalized using a hierarchy. If the selling

---

[300] BROWN/GOOLSBEE (2000) found that the Internet has the power to significantly reduce consumer search costs by providing consumers with low-cost online price comparisons.

process can not be controlled because the technology to protect the IPRs is too weak (watermarks, DRM systems) the case is different. This would mean that people can freeride by copying the music track without paying for it. Since optimal integration depends upon the IPR regime and potential free-riding problems, Public Good Theory is useful to learn more about this crucial facet of the analysis. Public good theory can also contribute to a better understanding of the specific product characteristics in the media sector and can help to analyze different internalization mechanisms.

4.3.4   (Re-)Privatizing public goods

In addition, Public Good Theory borrowed from public finance can potentially provide another theoretical motivation for the change of firm boundaries in the media sector. Like in the model of double marginalization, a market failure occurs that induces the shift in firm boundaries.

This shift is related to certain product characteristics of music. As shown in the beginning, music can be described as an information good. An important characteristic of an information good is the similarity to a public good. The consumption process of a public good is marked by a lack of rivalry and a lack of excludability.[302] Lack of rivalry means that the good can be consumed by several individuals at the same time and/or several times by the same consumer.[303] The lack of excludability is a state where potential consumers can not be excluded from the consumption of a good for technical reasons, at least not at a reasonable cost. They can be classified with the typology in the table below:

---

[301] See CARTER (1998).
[302] See SAMUELSON (1954), MUSGRAVE (1959).
[303] Non-rivalry means that the marginal cost of additional users consuming the good is low or zero because consumption utility for the other individual is independent of fellow consumers, see MUSGRAVE/MUSGRAVE (1989), p. 43.

Table 7: Public Good Topology

Classification of Goods (in brackets: internalization mechanism)	Rivalry	No Rivalry
Excludability	Private Goods, e.g. physical retail goods (market mechanism)	Semi-public/Club Goods, e.g. squash courts (user clubs, subscription models, cooperatives)
No Excludability	Semi-public/Allmende Goods, e.g. the global commons[304] (pollution certificate trading[305], Pigou tax[306])	Public Goods/Collective Goods, e.g. external security of a country (governmental provision of good, franchise bidding when contestable)

Source: own table.

Private goods are most common. A typical example is food. Exclusion is possible, e.g. by storing the food in a safe place. Since food can be eaten only once, rivalry in consumption is high.

Public goods are goods like public defense, where everybody can benefit from the provision of the good without reducing the consumption benefits for his fellow users. The classical example of external security/public defense in a defined territory shows that exclusion from the benefits of this good is not feasible. The intermediate forms are particularly meaningful in the context of this analysis and analyzed in the following paragraphs.

Club goods[307] have a production cost structure with high fixed cost and very low marginal cost of usage. If marginal cost pricing is applied the price for a one-time usage of the good should be reflecting its marginal cost, i.e. be very low or zero. The problem is that the cost of production is not equal to zero. Squash courts are a good example: construction costs are high compared to the cost of using the court once. Rivalry in consumption does not exist except for peak-time access because players can use the court sequentially without destroying the good.

---

[304] For instance, global fishing grounds.

[305] Pollution certificate trading internalizes a negative externality by introducing a certificate that entitles the polluter (originator of an externality) to pollute. The value of the certificate reflects the cost of the externality. See FRITSCH ET AL (1996), p. 111-113.

[306] See PIGOU (1938). A Pigou tax is a tax (subsidy) that internalizes a negative (positive) externality by taxing (subsidizing) the activity of the originator of the externality such that the social and private cost (utility) of the activity is equal. Again, see FRITSCH ET AL (1996), p. 94-97 for a good overview.

[307] See BUCHANAN (1965) for the foundations of the Theory of Clubs.

According to the Theory of Clubs the optimal pricing model is to charge marginal cost (low or zero) and raise the necessary financial resources to construct the court via a fixed club fee.[308]

Allmende goods face the problem of excessive usage. An individual that consumes the good induces costs but can not be excluded from this consumption act. A common example are global fishing grounds where everybody would be better off by restricting his usage or paying the equivalent of the cost induced. Since exclusion is not feasible, free-riding is the optimal solution from the individual's point of view.

Public Good Theory is a useful framework to demonstrate the effects of ICT. The impact of ICT affected both attributes rivalry and excludability of music as a good. ICT innovations in digital reproduction technology of music thereby severely changed music as a product.

Tangible CDs can be copied to other tangible CDs via CD burners or can be encoded into a digital intangible data file using the MP3 algorithm.[309] This process eliminates the characteristic of rivalry in consumption for this type of good. A music CD used to be a good with reduced rivalry because more than one consumer can listen to it simultaneously. The CD is also a durable good, i.e. is not destroyed with the consumption act. However, the physical storage medium, the recording, has traditionally been needed for the consumption act.[310] This made simultaneous consumption of the same music at two different places recording impossible without acquiring another copy of the original recording. An unresolved question is the necessity of own data media like CDs if the consumption procedure can be pursued without owning the physical medium.[311] Acquiring another copy means compensating the IPR owner for this additional copy.[312] With CD burners and MP3 technology, the content of a CD is no longer linked to one physical item but can be copied, shared and exchanged at very little

---

[308] The club solution can be applied to all goods with the described cost structure. Examples are railroad tracks or car sharing clubs.

[309] The data file is often compressed using MP3 technology, i.e. reduced to a small fraction of its original size in order to make music dissemination, i.e. exchange via email, file-swapping networks etc. easier.

[310] We abstract from audio tape copies of CDs and records because this case is different. Their quality and durability is limited and can not be compared to digital clones in form of ripped CDs or swapped MP3 files.

[311] If subscription models like Napster II become the predominant music consumption technique the necessity to physically own the music vanishes. This has often been characterized as the "jukebox in the sky" or "celestial jukebox", see e.g. LEHMAN BROTHERS (2001).

or even no cost. The copy of a music track is as good as the original track, i.e. a good can be consumed simultaneously by several consumers at different places with only one or even no purchase necessary, i.e. the good does not show rivalry in consumption.

Excludability is also affected. Both types of digital reproduction technology, CD burners to produce digital clones of original CDs and P2P networks like Napster, are now starting to take away excludability from goods that already have no rivalry in consumption. This happens via reducing reproduction and distribution costs. Both, the marginal costs of reproduction and distribution jointly protected copyrights by safeguarding excludability in consumption. Without a control mechanism for the exchange of copyrights like in the pirate versions music swapping technology (the old Napster system, Gnutella[313]) excludability is no longer guaranteed. Everybody can obtain the good for free without taking something away from others.

This would turn music into a public good. Excludability could be restored by increasing IPR protection efficiency. IPR protection can be realized technically by implementing Digital Rights Management (DRM) systems. This technology enables the owner of an IPR to charge for the use of the IPR in his possession.[314] Alternative IPR protection mechanisms are digital watermarks. The same applies for CD copying. Copying the physical CD without the consent of the IPR owner eliminates excludability. A regime that controls and charges the reproduction of copyrighted CDs would restore excludability. In the public good matrix, the structural changes in the music industry can be described as follows:

---

[312] In fact, there are two principal intellectual property rights in the music industry: the rights to the work itself (the composition) like the music sheets (typically owned by the publishing company) and the performance and duplication rights (typically owned by the record label) see VOGEL (2001), p. 138.

[313] Gnutella, Grokster, Morpheus, KaZaa and a vast variety of unnamed other services are technologies that allows file sharing over the internet without a central server see, IFPI (2002a). Kazaa is incorporated in Vanuatu, a country that has a tradition of non-cooperation with law enforcers from other countries as noted by WALTER (1990), p.189. This makes it extremely difficult or almost impossible to control or oversee the provider of this copying technology.

[314] The major types of DRM systems that can be used to charge for IPRs are explained in appendix VI.

Table 8: Public Good Topology applied to Recent Developments in the Music Industry

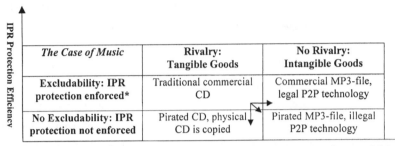

The Case of Music	Rivalry: Tangible Goods	No Rivalry: Intangible Goods
Excludability: IPR protection enforced*	Traditional commercial CD	Commercial MP3-file, legal P2P technology
No Excludability: IPR protection not enforced	Pirated CD, physical CD is copied	Pirated MP3-file, illegal P2P technology

* no PC-based physical CD copying / MP3 file swapping only with DRM. Development of digital reproduction technology

Source: own table.

Based on the product characteristics of music and the different environmental forces affecting these characteristics (ICT, IPR regime) an optimal consumption model/business model is illustrated in table 9. Given that IPRs can be protected via DRM systems, efficiency in terms of marginal cost pricing can be realized by implementing subscription services,[315] and music files could be distributed online using the club model. A fixed monthly payment by the club users is charged in order to compensate the creator of the IPRs. Since marginal costs of producing an additional copy of the music file are (almost) zero the flat monthly fee is the only charge within the subscription service solution. The price for a single download/copy is equal to its marginal cost, i.e. equal to zero.

Table 9: Optimal Business Model according to Public Good Topology

The Case of Music [internalization mechanism]	Rivalry: Tangible Goods	No Rivalry: Intangible Goods
Excludability: IPR protection enforced*	Traditional commercial CD sold in highstreet stores	Online Music Retailers [flat rate subscription, clubs fee for downloads]
No Excludability: IPR protection not enforced	Traditional commercial CD sold in highstreet stores [hardware tax]	Music market failure or [hardware tax + club fee]

Development of digital reproduction technology

Source: own table.

---

[315] This implies that further copying of the acquired file is technically impossible. Otherwise users could acquire a file at marginal cost and give the copy to other users for free.

The public good argument from the literature is a classical case of market failure. The quantity of the public good produced by the market is insufficient or zero. The outcome is determined by the IPR protection regime. Increasing use of the MP3 algorithm, i.e. rising digitalization, signifies that either a working IPR regime helps music companies to claim their property rights on media products or the market will break down. Given that IPRs are protected, the outcome would be a subscription model or a music user club.

If the IPR protection is insufficient, alternative internalization methods are needed. Taxing Internet equipment could be one possibility to internalize the externality generated by digitalization with a Pigou tax.[316] If digitalization of music can be contained, the distribution model will be the sale of physical CDs. From an efficiency point of view, IPR protection will determine the optimal provision model for music. The externality from illegal physical CD ripping[317] could be internalized with a hardware tax on CD burners. The distribution of the tax revenues is a task for future research on optimal distribution rules. Technically, it can contribute to a redistribution of the economic rents generated with music copyrights.[318]

Since the media industry will not tolerate the losses[319] induced by the market failure situation (public good outcome) in the long run, two possibilities remain: vertical integration or a two-paired tariff.[320] Under certain conditions, a two-paired tariff (here: a subscription-based pricing model in the form of a commercial subscription-based online music user club)[321] could lead to the same efficiency result as integration. Information problems can complicate the implementation of the two-paired tariff. There are various sources of information problems, e.g. when the retailer has private information about final demand or uncertainty in the form of insufficient property rights protection. Without a working IPR protection regime the contracting solution using the market via a two-paired tariff (i.e. a club fee) is not feasible.

---

[316] The rules for splitting up the collected tax revenues are still unclear but tax collecting is feasible and working in other media markets: VOGEL (2001) notes that videocassettes sold to rental stores include a proportion of "first-sale" rights, i.e. a compensation for the IPR use by rental store customers who rent the videocassette. The same applies in analogy for buyers of copying machines like universities.

[317] This means to copy an audio CD on CD-ROM using a PC.

[318] Today, artists receive only a small stake of the rents, see LEHMAN BROTHERS (2001). The biggest stakes are commanded by the music publishing houses that usually belong to the record label.

[319] The Recording Industry Association of America (RIAA) estimated 1.3m illegally recorded CDs in 2001 (a 133% increase on the same period in 2000), see THE ECONOMIST (2001b).

[320] A definition is given in FRITSCH ET AL (1996), p. 176: a two-paired tariff is a tariff that consists of a fixed fee (club fee) to pay for the fixed costs involved in the production of the respective good and a small fee per usage that compensates for the low marginal cost of usage. See also KIRSCH (1997), p. 171-178.

With no IPR protection in place, content distribution in the age of P2P technology is out of control. Hence, the exogenous shock of new ICT in the form of P2P keeps on transforming more and more private information goods into public goods. Even if there are copyright protection laws, it might not be feasible to enforce them for technical or political[322] reasons.

DRM Systems are not a big success today but might facilitate contracting out the distribution channel for intangible media products that can be exchanged easily among consumers without paying the copyright holder. If media companies are in a situation with weak copyright control or anticipate insufficient copyright protection technology and protection laws in the future, integration would be a rational and efficient step for them. If commercial use of DRM technology is a success, market based forms of music distribution will be feasible, e.g. a subscription model like Napster II (the club good/subscription model). The efficiency of DRM systems, the strength of the rule of law prohibiting physical CD-copying, will determine the business model and the revenue model for the music industry of the future.

Hence, the theoretical motivation for firm boundary change in the global music and media markets based on Public Good Theory is not unambiguous. However, the theory is useful to enhance our understanding of subscription services for digital goods distributed over the Internet. Firm try to (re-)privatize their media products in order to avoid the loss of IPRs. By applying Public Good Theory I identified IPR protection, or more exactly enforced IPR protection, as the key variable influencing the selection of the optimal business model. The interaction between IPR protection, its enforcement, and ICT are analyzed in the following paragraph. The two central questions are (i) if there is a (harmful) effect of ICT of selling IPRs, and (ii) if this effect is reduced by legal IPR protection. Since this is an empirical question I use an empirical analysis of a panel dataset of recorded music sales to find answers.

---

[321] This club could also be organized as a cooperative. STAATZ (1983) points out the similarity between Buchanan's clubs and (agricultural) cooperatives.

[322] Enforcement could be hindered by national sovereignty of countries with different IPR protection concepts.

4.4 Intellectual Property Rights Protection as a Determinant of Media Firm Boundaries

4.4.1 The Nature of Intellectual Property Rights

As shown in the previous analysis, the future shape of media firm boundaries is hypothesized to crucially depend upon the IPR protection regime of a business environment and its enforcement. Most media products are information goods that involve a substantial amount of IPRs. Protection mechanisms for IPRs are necessary to provide incentives for the production of information goods. Without copyright protection individuals would not be encouraged to produce certain unique or creative works as noted by LANDES/POSNER (1989, p. 332).

Public Good Analysis demonstrated that in a market that lacks IPR protection and/or its enforcement the result would be a market failure because of free rider problems. From an welfare point of view, there is a downside to IPR protection.[323] A copyright, i.e. a protected IPR, is the guarantee to be the only one that reproduces a good, i.e. a monopoly right. The quantity of the goods produced with the IPRs in an unprotected situation would be greater than in the restricted situation. The avoidance of the competitive situation in which everybody can use the IPRs leads inevitably to monopoly rents and to a deadweight loss. The monopoly rents contain consumer surplus that is redistributed to the IPR owner.

SCOTCHMER (1991) notes that the deadweight loss in terms of welfare is enlarged by second generation producers who use the restricted information as their input (dynamic loss). Although the monopoly situation induces an economic loss, the situation in which IPRs are not protected is worse.[324] Without an IPR protection regime there would not be a rent at all as shown at the beginning (free rider problem). The value of the copyright is equal to the discounted value of the positive net economic rents for the duration of the copyright.[325] The duration of the copyright is usually the artists life plus 50 years for the case of music.[326]

The monopoly distortions lead to a tradeoff between inefficient underproduction without IPR protection and underutilization with IPR protection. NORDHAUS (1969), SCHERER (1972), and TANDON (1982) developed a theory of optimal patents in order to determine the optimal

---

[323] See GILBERT/SHAPIRO (1990).
[324] Since the main insights of this article can be summarized verbally, I do not provide a figure.
[325] See LANDES/POSNER (1989).

amount of IPR protection in terms of welfare. The result is a function of various variables including the reduction in demand for originals compared to its impact on total consumption and consumer preference for product variety is analyzed by JOHNSON (1985).

The literature on the interaction between different business strategies which includes the drawing of firm boundaries and IPR protection regimes is relatively scant. BENKLER (2002) delivers a model to show that the welfare analysis of IPR regimes needs to include the divergent effects on different business strategies. This means that an IPR protection regime influences welfare via its effect on the organization of information production (in this case music production).[327] I take the reverse perspective by giving theoretical rationales of optimal business strategies in a distinct and given IPR environment, i.e. to evaluate different organizational designs of firms operating in a distinct business environment.

The eclectic theoretical analysis performed in chapter 4.3 pointed out that the crucial variable to understand the relationship between firm boundaries and ICT in the media sector is IPR protection. In the following paragraph, I add an international perspective to this issue and focus especially on the interaction between ICT and IPR protection.

4.4.2 An International Perspective on the Interaction of Information Technology and Intellectual Property Rights Protection

The synopsis of theoretical approaches to media firm organization shows that the efficient organizational structure of firms selling media products seems to be affected by two important environmental determinants. The ICT environment determines the efficient distribution channel, i.e. to sell either physical CDs or digital MP3 files or both. The public good topology developed earlier can help to categorize these changes. The second important environmental determinant is the IPR regime. If we assume that the IPRs of music products can be protected with a DRM system a commercial subscription service for music downloads would make sense. If IPRs cannot be protected this way, music firms could refer to more crude solutions like hardware taxes etc.

---

[326] See BESEN/RASKIND (1991), p. 10.

IPR regimes and ICT environments are not independent of each other. IPR regimes can be contingent on the ICT environment of a country. The link between the two environmental variables is the enforcement of the IPR regimes. It is difficult to control the illegal copying of CDs with CD burners but it is almost not feasible to control the swapping of music files via the Internet.[328]

Both, changes in the IPR regimes and changes in the ICT environment determine the efficient organizational shape of the global music firms. The interaction between the technological side (ICT environment) and the legal side (IPR protection) is an important determinant of the whole process. Studies of the interaction between innovative and regulatory forces in the financial sector describe an analogous problem.

The phenomenon that the regulation of financial innovation always lagged behind the innovation rate has been extensively analyzed under the term "regulatory dialectic".[329] The fact that a ban on the most prominent music file exchange (Napster) spurred innovation in form of the creation of alternative music file exchanges demonstrates the dialectical character of this process: the design of the regulatory regime has to be compatible with the technological capabilities of the regulated subjects. Otherwise the regulatory act can produce new technological innovations aiming to bypass or circumvent the existing legal framework. This dialectic process is described in the following figure:

---

[327] For example, strong IPR protection laws trigger a concentrated production structure of homogeneous information and less usage of the protected information. The theoretical analysis by BENKLER (2002) shows that this concentration process in the industry structure ceteris paribus leads to negative welfare effects.
[328] IFPI (2002b).

Figure 17: Regulatory Dialectic between IPR Protection and ICT Innovation

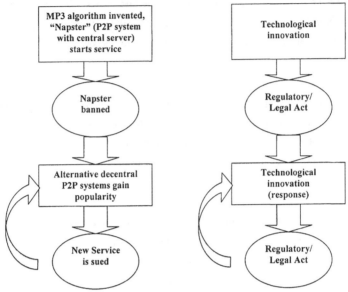

Source: own figure.

International legal action regarding IPR protection issues is still quite slow. This further increases the dialectical character of the interaction between the IPR and the ICT environment. The analysis of the interaction between ICT and IPR protection showed that enforceability of an IPR protection scheme is crucial. The main goal of an IPR regime is to ban illegal copying of intellectual property. A landmark in IPR legislation has been the Berne Convention of 1886. The treaty grants the exclusive economic rights to a creative work's translation, reproduction, performance, and adaptation to the artist.[330]

In the following decades, the Berne Convention served as a foundation for further IPR protection legislation. All multinational legal efforts in the field of IPR protection have been extensions of the international treaty of the Berne Convention.[331] Two central pieces of legislation have been created with the intention to translate the content of the Berne Convention to the new ICT environment by the WIPO:[332] the so-called WIPO "Internet

---

[329] See KANE (1981).
[330] See GALLAGHER (2001).
[331] The convention has been revised in 1914, 1928, 1948, 1967, and 1971.
[332] The WIPO is a sub-organization of the WTO (World Trade Organization) specializing in IPR issues.

treaties", i.e. the WIPO Copyright Treaty (WCT) and the WIPO Performances and Phonograms Treaty (WPPT).[333] The WIPO treaties have been created in December 1996 and set a standard for online copyright laws around the world. Both, WCT and WPPT have been adopted by a minimum number of countries (30) and thereby became international law.[334] Obviously, the effect of the WPPT on CD sales is not directly linked to the time of ratification but depends upon the (independent) decision of the respective countries to enforce the spirit of the treaty irrespective of its ratification.

The interaction between these two environmental forces will remain an important determinant for the efficient structure of media firm boundaries. Facing rapid technological change, in particular in the way we consume music, the international legal framework is likely to be unable to cope with the velocity of change in the ICT environment that can be observed in the last decade.

4.4.3 Empirical Analysis

The theoretical analysis so far clarified that IPR protection is a crucial factor in the relationship between media firm boundaries and ICT. Theory suggests that media firms seem to insource in order to avoid IPR leakage induced by ICT. This section contains an empirical test of the relationship between ICT and IPRs. In addition, the role of IPR protection is analyzed regarding its effectiveness to influence the impact of ICT on IPRs. The relationship between ICT and IPRs has to be operationalized in order to test the ability of certain ICTs to increase the risk of loosing IPRs because of piracy.

I use the revenues generated with the sale of an IPR-intense product (recorded music) as a subject of analysis. Therefore I estimate the impact of different types of ICT (PCs and the Internet) on the sales generated with recorded music and control the analysis for alternative determinants of music sales. I also include measures of IPR protection in order to analyze the role of the IPR protection environment in this relationship. After elucidating the relationship between ICT, IPRs, and IPR enforcement, the theoretical rationales for media firm boundary

---

[333] The 'trade-related aspects of intellectual property rights' (TRIPS) agreement of 1995 basically supplements the WIPO Conventions on intellectual property, the WTO action.
[334] The WCT of 1996 entered into force on March 6, 2002 after Gabon became the 30th party of the treaty. The WPPT followed on May 20, 2002.

change can be evaluated. Given that IPRs can be enforced, media firm boundaries could be drawn according to the club model, i.e. using integrated online distribution designs protected by IPR protection.

The proceeding is as follows: instead of measuring organizational change with a vertical integration index based on accounting data the impact of ICT on media firm boundaries is tested indirectly via an analysis of ICT impact on IPR protection. In order to examine the effect of a changing ICT environment on the degree of IPR protection worldwide sales figures of total recorded music (TRM)[335] per capita in different countries are examined with special regard to the impact of PC and Internet penetration. Again, the variance in the institutional environment especially in terms of ICT penetration is used to explain a particular phenomenon in the business sector, in this case the development of sales values for recorded music (VALTRMPC).

As in chapter three, ICT penetration is measured with the number of Internet hosts per capita. I add a second ICT measure (penetration with personal computers) in order to account for the peculiarities of the media sector. Copyright infringements occur because of two main reasons: music file exchange in Internet-based file sharing communities (proxied with the number of Internet hosts per capita (IH)) and via copying/burning of CDs using PCs (proxied by penetration with PCs (PCPEN)). Both are expected to show a negative impact on music sales.

The analysis is controlled for determinants of music sales other than ICT. Obvious determinants with a positive influence on TRM sales include the availability of CD players (percentage of households that possess a CD player, CDPLHH), economic growth (real GDP growth, REALGDPGW), the economic development of a country (GDP per capita, GDPPC), and the availability of legal ways to acquire recorded music (number of record shops per capita, NORECSTOPC). The quality of the institutions in which the music sales take place are measured with the POLCON variable already used in chapter three of this study.

Music sales data is available from the EUROMONITOR database from 29 countries over 5 years starting 1996. The sample countries are shown in appendix VII. I have CD sales data

---

[335] I use the amount of total recorded music instead of CD sales in order to eclipse substitution effects between different formats of recorded music.

for 6 years and 45 countries, i.e. 270 data points. For 16 countries and for 1995 data was unavailable for most of the independent variables reducing my sample to a sample size of 145. Complete data is available for the desired time range 1996-2000 in 29 countries. Descriptive statistics are given in the following table.

Table 10: Descriptive Statistics

	Min	Max	Mean	SD
VALTRMPC	0.00	61.40	18.6607	17.0977
GDPPC	466.90	36508.60	14898.6645	11251.7434
REALGDPGW	-13.10	10.90	3.3069	3.5974
IH	13.20	300976.58	21680.9661	37204.9314
PCPEN	1.50	137.50	28.5804	26.8590
CDPLHH	0.90	87.40	31.9607	28.2462
NORECSTOPC	0.41	1068.62	150.4199	219.0613
POLCON	0.00	0.59	0.3974	0.1518

Following the proceeding of chapter three, I use a panel regression design to detect the influence of my ICT variables on the sales of recorded music (VALTRMPC). Therefore, I pursue a fixed effect panel regression.[336] The results are reported in table below.

Table 11: Test Results (Media)[337]

Variables	(1)	(2)	(3)	(4)	(5)
GDPPC	0.001396	0.0014	0.000888	0.001413	0.000103
	(6.31)***	(6.37)***	(3.96)***	(6.46)***	(5.17)***
REALGDPGW	0.06547	0.061172	0.108281	0.081854	0.120
	(0.71)	(0.67)	(1.30)	(0.90)	(1.69)*
IH	-0.00004	-0.00004	-0.00003	-0.00004	-0.00003
	(-2.59)**	(-2.61)**	(-1.66)	(-2.41)**	(-1.54)
PCPEN	-0.19644	-0.19597	1.006782	-0.11748	0.873
	(-3.60)***	(-3.61)***	(1.99)**	(-1.47)	(1.91)*
CDPLHH	-0.09949	-0.09891	-0.14914	-0.14094	-0.174
	(-1.15)	(-1.15)	(-1.75)*	(-1.54)	(-1.74)*
NORECSTOPC	0.01694	0.017323	0.014388	0.024105	0.020438
	(0.78)	(0.80)	(0.70)	(1.10)	(1.06)
POLCON	-1.40292				
	(-0.30)				
IH*WPPTINV			-0.0001		-0.00009
			(-2.94)***		(-2.55)**
PCPEN*WPPTINV			-1.17918		-1.25453
			(-2.34)**		(-2.24)**
IH*POLCONINV				0.000375	0.000004
				(1.30)	(0.07)
PCPEN*POLCONINV				-0.28208	-1.151
				(-1.81)*	(-0.46)
IH*POLCONINV*WPPTINV					-0.00028
					(-0.46)
PCPEN*POLCONINV*WPPTINV					-0.166
					(-1.35)
Adjusted R2	0.9747	0.9747	0.9796	0.9755	0.9800
NT	145	145	145	145	145
Model	FE	FE	FE	FE	FE

---

[336] The Hausman test suggests the fixed effect setup in this case. For a discussion of the different panel data regression model see chapter three.

The results indicate that both measures of ICT penetration show a negative impact on music sales figures. PC penetration appears to be the main negative determinant of the sales figures.[338] As expected, wealthier countries show significantly higher music sales per capita. The penetration with CD players shows an unanticipated but insignificant negative relationship. The number of record shops has the expected sign but no significance. The political environment in form of POLCON shows no significant impact. POLCON is dropped in regression (2) without inducing much change in the regression.

The theoretical analysis pointed out that the degree of IPR protection is an important moderating factor in the relationship between IPR and ICT.[339] In order to include IPR protection, which is considered to be an important determinant of the business environment in which the music sales take place, I use the WPPT treaty mentioned earlier. The treaty contains legislation targeted at IPR issues in the new ICT environment affecting the sales process of media and music products.[340] Since this variable has no variation over time I use a sample split to analyze its impact. I construct an inverse dummy variable (WPPTDUMINV) with the value 0 for all WPPT-countries and the value 1 for all other countries.[341] In a second step, I create an interaction dummy in order to test the differences between these two groups of countries by multiplying the ICT-variables with the inverse WPPT-dummy (IH*WPPTINV and PCPEN*WPPTINV respectively). The results of this sample split are given in regression (3).

Regression (3) shows that in countries that have not started to upgrade their copyright legislation using the WPPT treaty, both ICT measures show a significant harmful effect. In countries that have joined the treaty there is no harmful effect of ICT on the dependent

[337] Figure in parentheses are t statistics (two-tailed tests). *, **, and *** denote significance at the 10%, 5%, and 1% levels respectively. Country dummies are not reported for brevity.

[338] An increase of one percentage point in PC penetration reduces music sales per capita by 20 cents of an US-Dollar.

[339] Depending upon the degree of IPR protection a certain business model is appropriate. As shown before, IPR protected business environments allow subscription/club distribution models for digital media goods. In contrast, business environments without IPR protection lead to the public good outcome with the associated media market breakdown.

[340] The treaty was negotiated at the beginning of the analyzed time period in 1996. The minimum number of countries ratified the treaties in 2002. Despite the fact that the implementation process is not fully completed in all member countries it is reasonable to assume that the ratifying status of a country in 2002 is a proxy for its IPR policy. Hence, the 2002 status is used to reflect the attitude towards online IPR protection during the analyzed time period. Other IPR measures that could have been used for a sample split (Ginarte-Park Index, see GINARTE/PARK (1997)) have the advantage of creating sub-samples of more equal size but do not focus on the Internet as a threat to IPR protection.

variable. PC penetration seems to be even driving music sales in WPPT-countries. The results support the interpretation that loss of music revenues is significantly lower in countries that follow the WIPO action. PCs penetration changes into a positive influence on music sales which might be a spurious correlation. Hence, the ICT threat to music sales seems to be minimized by using modern IPR legislation.

Although POLCON does not show an impact that differs significantly from zero there might be a difference in the impact of the WPPT-variable on the relationship between ICT and music sales. To shed light on the interactions between WPPT-membership status and the political regime I construct another interaction variable that consists of both, POLCON and WPPT-status.

Since POLCON has little within-group variation, I dichotomize my sample in terms of the POLCON score. I use a dummy-version that takes the value 1 for countries with above-the-mean POLCON scores and 0 for all other countries, and a dummy variable POLCONINV with the inverse values of the original dummy. I run another regression (not reported here) with both, WPPT interaction dummies and POLCON interaction dummies for IH and PCPEN. The values for the new dummy variables IH*POLCONINV and PCPEN*POLCONINV can be interpreted as the impact of ICT in countries with low POLCON scores. The results are insignificant: both POLCON interaction dummies show an insignificant positive and negative sign respectively.[342] The two WPPT-interaction dummies (IH*WPPTINV and PCPEN*WPPTINV) keep their negative sign.

Dropping the WPPT-interaction dummies and including POLCON-interaction dummies leads to an interesting result. Neglecting the impact of WPPT-status, high POLCON-regimes show a negative impact of Internet penetration (IH) on music sales compared to low POLCON-regimes as reported in regression (4). The impact of PC penetration (PCPEN) is reverse: PCPEN depresses music sales only in low POLCON-regimes but not those with high POLCON-scores. A possible interpretation of this finding is that PC-based copyright

---

[341] Appendix VII contains a list of the WPPT member countries.
[342] The original ICT variables show an insignificant positive sign.

infringements occur predominantly in countries with a low-quality political system while P2P-based music downloads take place mainly in more developed political regimes.[343]

I also test double interaction dummies for a joint effect of WPPT and POLCON by multiplying both, POLCON-dummies with the (inverse) WPPT dummy.[344] I use the new variables to isolate the effect of my ICT variables on WPPT-nonmember countries (WPPTINV value of 1) with low POLCON-scores (POLCONINV value of 1). The results for the double interaction dummies are insignificant. The new pair of dummies show the marginal effect added by a low POLCON score in WPPT-non-member countries to the impact of ICT on music sales. Neither of my ICT variables shows a marginal impact added by POLCON to the WPPT-moderated ICT-music sales relationship and vice versa. The negative ICT-effect in the non-WPPT countries remains highly significant as reported in regression (5).[345] A plausible interpretation for this result can be that – regardless of the political regime – WPPT-membership is decisive for the formation of a transaction environment that saves IPRs from being pirated while the political regime influences the dominant type of piracy.[346] Without membership, politics does not make a difference in this case.

I also performed the usual robustness checks.[347] In order to avoid that the results are driven by some extreme observations that have a greater influence on model fit than others I analyzed the residuals. I did a robustness check by using Cook's D as an influence statistics.[348] Cook's D measures the change in the parameter estimates caused by deleting each observation.[349] D-values that exceed one are considered to be influential. Although there are no such values in my sample I eliminate the two observations with maximal D-values.[350] Again, the result for the detrimental impact of ICT in non-WPPT countries remains significant. Hence, the results

---

[343] To assess the full complexity of this relationship more empirical research is necessary but beyond the scope of this dissertation.

[344] This leads to the variables IH*POLCONINV*WPPTINV and PCPEN*POLCONINV*WPPTINV.

[345] Internet penetration and PC penetration are negatively correlated with music sales in non-WPPT countries on a 1% and 5% significance level respectively.

[346] An additional analysis with interaction dummies for OECD membership yielded no significant results.

[347] Durbin-Watson statistics for the regressions show acceptable values of around 1.5. The residual plot indicates no signs of heteroskedasticity.

[348] See JOBSON (1992b), p. 298.

[349] Cook's D uses the sum of squared distances between the two lines (with and without observation) as a measure of influence.

[350] There are two observations with D-values greater than 0.1. This might be related to unexpected music sales figures in Japan in 2000 and The Netherlands in 1996. In fact, IFPI (2001, p. 97) reports that some exceptional major album releases by local artists and a successful series of mid-price millennial compilations that temporary boosted Japan's record sales in 2000.

are robust regarding outliers. The negative impact of ICT on music sales is significantly lowered in WPPT-governed environments compared to the WPPT-non-member countries. This is valid with and without the two observations on a 5% significance level.

In summary, the empirical results support the theoretical findings of this chapter. The sales process of products that involve a large proportion of IPRs is affected significantly by the ICT environment in which it takes place. The consequences of high ICT penetration are different: obviously, media firms operating in countries with good availability of ICT face difficulties to protect their IPRs. IPR protection – at least in the case of WIPO action – can help to reduce this problem. According to the empirical analysis, good political institutions do not improve the situation in non-WPPT countries. The future development will crucially depend upon the success of the WIPO legislation and the ability of a country to enforce these new IPR laws.

4.5   Conclusion

Both, theory and evidence on ICT impact on media firms suggest that IPR protection is a central variable in this relationship. The theoretical synopsis provided a rationale for the organizational response of global media firms we observe. Incomplete Contract Theory, Industrial Organization, and Public Good Theory provide compatible insights into the changes in firm boundaries although from different perspectives. As shown in this chapter, they all can offer useful answers to the question if integration and ownership of the media value chain from content production to the distribution stage returns some control to the media content owners.

IO Theory can help to understand the relation between market structure and industry organization in the media industry. Incomplete Contract Theory suggests that ICT improves markets and their efficiency by decreasing ex-ante transaction costs (like search cost) but seem to increase ex-post transaction cost (e.g. contract enforcement costs). Assuming that the ex-post transaction cost effects outweigh the ex-ante transaction cost reductions rising vertical integration in the media sector is an efficient strategic response. Public Good Theory is useful to integrate alternative internalization mechanisms into the analysis. Recent organizational innovations like subscription-based music consumption via P2P technology can be motivated in an existing theoretical context. In addition, it contributes to our understanding of club-like subscription-based distribution models.

The economic downturn in 2001 and 2002 showed that not all corporate architectures that were organized according to the integrated media firm rationale proved to be viable.[351] I will give two explanations for this observation. The first cause, might have been the general inefficiency of combining content with distribution, i.e. vertical integration in the media sector. The second and more convincing reason is a firm-specific effect. Obviously, not all media market firm boundary changes have produced efficient new firm boundaries. Network effects in the retail market might not have led to the necessary degree of market power that justifies vertical integration according to the double marginalization explanation.

The rationale for integration into online retail segments of the media value chain was based on market imperfections that occur because of lock-in effects. LIEBOWITZ (2002) argues that Internet-induced network effects had been overestimated. Hence market imperfections in downstream end-consumer online media markets proved to be less imperfect than expected. LIEBOWITZ (2002) notes that a lack of differentiation between different types of network effects had been the main cause for overestimation. Internet-induced network effects lead to two kinds of lock-in. The first type, 'soft lock-in' occurs when consumers face switching costs because of learning cost for a new technology ('self-incompatibility'). This type of lock-in is very common for many new products. The second type, 'strong lock-in' relates to situations where consumers face two different incompatible technological standards (external incompatibility). The second type would lead to a coordination failure and welfare losses because a superior technology is suppressed by a weaker first-mover technology.[352] According to LIEBOWITZ (2002) the second type of lock-in is very rare. This allows another interpretation of downstream integration in online media markets. Given that market imperfections were lower than expected by the strategic decision makers (during the overheated stock market), integration efforts into online retail segments of the media value chain were inefficient.

---

[351] THE ECONOMIST (2002b).
[352] Often cited examples are the VCR standard "VHS" and the QUERTY computer keyboard. Both are alleged to have laced competing technologies (that supposed to be superior) via reaching a critical mass of users.

As shown in the empirical tests, ICT penetration affects the rent streams generated with selling IPRs in the form of music but this effect can be reduced using IPR protection. The theoretical analysis depicted that IPR protection becomes more and more complex in the new ICT arena. If the regulatory dialectic can not be stopped it will become difficult for record companies to generate sales in the traditional way. The empirical study of recorded music sales showed that there is a negative impact of ICT on the business with recorded music. Given that the regulatory dialectic can be stopped (e.g. with a prudent implementation of WIPO legislation) and a functioning subscription service can be developed technically, music companies can react with an adaptation of their firm boundaries. A firm morphology with an integrated online distribution stage would be the efficient firm boundary response. In case of an unstopped regulatory dialectic music will resemble more and more a public good and require an alternative mechanism to monetize IPR, e.g. a hardware tax.[353]

Inefficient organizational structures affect performance in the long run. Media firms have to take into account the new ICT environment in order to create firm morphologies that are able to support the collection of IPR-related revenues. If music firms fail to regain control over the music distribution process and thereby protect their copyrights they will suffer performance decreases. Given that IPRs can be protected technologically (e.g. with DRM systems) and legally (under the WIPO treaties) firms have to adapt their boundaries appropriately. The subscription-model could be an appropriate organizational response.

However, the future shape of the music industry and the media industry as a whole will depend upon issues like the technical and legal efficiency of IPR protection. Media firm boundaries are determined by the new ICT environment in which rapid technological innovation meets politicians trying to shape this environment by producing and enforcing IPR laws. The future media firm will be the outcome of this regulatory dialectic.

In order to understand the impact of ICT on firm boundaries in a comprehensive way, a synopsis of the results from the media and the manufacturing sector is imperative. The

---

LIEBOWITZ/MARGOLIS (1990) doubt that these cases are examples for network-induced standard effects but an effect of weaker/stronger product technologies.

[353] Assuming that hardware tax solves the problem of IPR-related revenue collection, the distribution of the tax proceeds among the different members of the media value chain (content producer, content aggregator, content distributor) is still a question to be answered. The potential struggles among the recipients of the IPR-related revenues have to be prevented by comprehensive distribution rules.

purpose of this synopsis is to contribute to our understanding of the ICT dimension in today's business environment. In chapter five I provide this synopsis and draw some final conclusions.

5. Final Conclusion and Outlook

The impact of the new information and communication environment on firm boundaries seems to be ambivalent. The comparison of the manufacturing and the media sector indicates that the ICT shock has had a differential impact. Based on a comprehensive literature review (chapter two) I found empirical evidence that ICT contributes to the modularization of value-chains in the manufacturing sector (chapter three) but provides vertical integration incentives in the media sector (chapter four). The results are compared in the chapter 4.1. The findings for the media sector are not a caveat of chapter three but can be motivated using the TCE framework which is explained in chapter 4.2.

5.1   Comparison of Main Results

Chapter three presented tentative evidence for a 'move-to-the-market' in the manufacturing sector. Finding a transaction partner for transactions with commoditized products like components of mobile communication devices is easier and cheaper with new ICT. For instance, ICT provides the technical basis to create firm structures relying on contract manufacturing partners. The empirical results substantiate the view that ICT-supported lean production structures integrating intermediate goods from outside suppliers can replace the internal production of inputs. I demonstrated that variance in the institutional and technological firm environments induces organizational change in the manufacturing sector. In this industry, ICT predominantly helps to economize on ex-ante transaction costs like search costs because components and intermediate products are often standardized. Outsourcing seems to be a common phenomenon in the manufacturing sector on an aggregate level. Firms can operate ceteris paribus with slimmer organizations in terms of vertical integration in highly developed ICT environments compared to settings with less ICT.

In contrast, *chapter four* showed that ICT affects the media sector in a different way: I provided empirical evidence in line with different theoretical arguments that the increasing vertical integration degrees in the media sector can be associated to some extent with the spread of new ICT. There is a fundamental difference in the product characteristics of media and manufacturing products: in contrast to most physical products found in the manufacturing sector, media products dramatically change their characteristics as a result of new ICT. I provide empirical evidence in chapter four that in IPR non-protecting environments ICT can induce IPR loss. This IPR loss together with the technical and legal IPR protection efficiency influences organizational decisions by media firms. For example, new distribution forms allow media companies to sell their content (e.g. music) using own ICT-based distribution channels. Both, the theoretical and the empirical analysis indicate that the crucial determinant for the efficiency of vertically integrated media business models is the degree of IPR protection. International legal action by the WIPO influences the sales process of products that contain a large proportion of IPRs in a positive way. The outcome of the dialectical process between IPR infringement and IPR protection remains a field for future research.

The impact of ICT on firm boundaries in the manufacturing industry is different from the media industry. However, TCE can explain both wider firm boundaries in the media sector and narrower firm boundaries in the manufacturing sector.

5.2 Transaction Costs as a Motivation for Differences in Firm Boundary Change

I argue that the main reason for the differential impact of ICT on firm boundaries is related to transaction cost effects. Differentiating between different types of transaction cost might help to understand vertical integration decisions. The two principal types of transaction costs are ex-ante and ex-post transaction costs as shown in the following figure.

Figure 18: Transaction Cost Dimensions

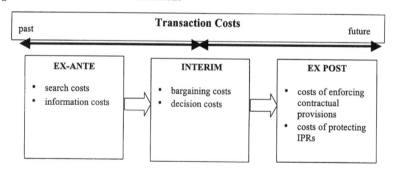

Source: Own figure based on WILLIAMSON (1985), p. 21.

This topology by WILLIAMSON (1985) uses a temporal structure to categorize the different types of transaction costs: ex-ante transaction costs accrue when individuals seek their transaction partners. Once the appropriate transaction partner is identified the transaction generates bargaining and decision costs, e.g. the cost of writing a contract that governs the transaction.[354] WILLIAMSON (1985, p. 21) states that the ex-post stage of a transaction evokes the "bonding costs of effecting secure commitments". WILLIAMSON (1991) argues that without protecting investments in knowledge, i.e. IPRs, the incentives to embed such investments in protective ex post governance structures increases.

The relevance of the different types of transaction costs depends upon the industry: ICT assists manufacturing firms primarily in saving ex-ante transaction costs. This leads to a 'move-to-the-market' according to my empirical study in chapter three. Due to the high degree of IPRs in its products the media sector faces essentially ex-post transaction cost increases that trigger a 'move-to-the-hierarchy' among media firms aiming to protect and control their content.

There is no denying that there are also ex-post transaction costs effects in the manufacturing sector, e.g. a reduction of small-number situations that reduces ex-post haggling over quasi-rents. There might also be ex-ante transaction costs effect for media firms but ex-post effects are dominant because of the intangible nature of most media products. However, my results are not contradictory to the interpretation that – on balance – the prevailing impact of ICT is the dominance of ex-ante transaction costs reductions in the manufacturing sector and increased ex-post transaction costs in the media sector. The impact of ICT on firm boundaries is described graphically in the following figure:

---

[354] Ex-interim transaction costs are neglected in the following for the sake of focussing on the characteristic differences between the manufacturing and the media industry.

Figure 19: ICT Impact on Firm Boundaries

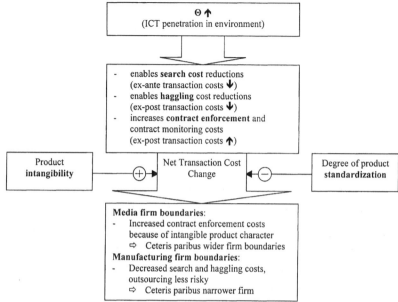

Source: own figure.

ICT induces variation in the institutional environment. This leads to diverging gross effects: ICT reduces search costs to find a transaction partner in the ex-ante stage of a transaction and can lead to lower haggling costs in its ex-post stage. At the same time, ICT can make it more difficult to enforce the terms of the contract agreed upon with a transaction partner as shown in the upper section of the figure. The typical product characteristics in an industry determine the net effect. The degree of product standardization and product intangibility (amount of IPRs involved) varies over industries. For manufacturing firms, ICT makes it easier to use decentralized, modular organizational structures that rely on the market as a governance mechanism. Market-based governance for transactions with typical manufacturing products is facilitated because of ICT which makes *firm boundaries* ceteris paribus *narrower* in the *manufacturing sector*. In the media sector, contract enforcement problems prevail. ICT in a scenario without IPR protection subverts the rent streams generated with the sale of intangible media products. This leads to an increase of hierarchical transaction governance used by media firms to regain/keep control over their rent streams from selling IPRs. Hence, ceteris paribus *wider firm boundaries* can be observed in the *media industry*.

5.3 Outlook

This dissertation does not intend to provide the organizational panacea for the new information and communication environment. The long-term viability of slim manufacturing firms and integrated media firms that emerged at the turn of the millennium is still unclear. TCE only teaches us that firm boundaries are shaped and reshaped constantly: firms with the best fit of business organization and business environment will probably succeed. Hence, the optimal proportion of market-based and hierarchical governance is a function of the institutional environment that varies both over time and between countries.

The analysis pursued here relies on different theoretical foundations with a special emphasis on TCE-based research. The comparison between the manufacturing and the media sector shows that TCE provides a rationale to better understand changing firm boundaries in both sectors. Consequently, TCE is – in the light of the results – a good scientific lens to look at the organizational impact of ICT. In particular, TCE broadens our understanding of the differences in ICT-induced firm boundary changes across different sectors and different institutional environments. TCE is particularly useful for (empirical) studies looking at the impact of institutional variation on firms that is induced by using international datasets. Bearing in mind the theta-approach by WILLIAMSON (1991), shifts in transaction governance can be both theorized and operationalized for empirical testing purposes using TCE.

To sum it up, TCE helps to rationalize the way human beings organize their economic activity by providing a convincing frame of reference that leads to powerful insights. TCE as a scientific framework is also extensible and almost timeless: the new ICT environment has changed firm boundaries but the fundamental explanations of organizational patterns gained from TCE are still valid.

How will technology influence the shape of the company of the future? The answer to this question is beyond the explanatory power of my dissertation. However, the answer will be determined by two main factors: the theories we use and the nature of the technological shock that occurs. The question remains to be answered but nevertheless I will draw one final conclusion and thereby follow SHAPIRO/VARIAN (1999, p.1): "Technology changes. Economic laws do not."

APPENDICES

Appendix I: Literature synopsis

Author   **Central results**

Determinants of firm boundaries

MONTEVERDE/TEECE (1982)
First empirical analysis of vertical integration determinants based on TCE arguments finding that higher asset specificity increased the likelihood of vertical integration compared to market procurement

CAVES/BRADBURD (1988)
Small-numbers bargaining, lock-in effects, and the necessity to commonly own intangible assets are drivers of vertical integration.

MASTEN (1984)
The likelihood of vertical integration is increased by asset specificity: the degree of component complexity and design specificity, i.e. the degree of component customization, are significant and positively related to vertical integration.

MACDONALD (1985)
Vertical integration is preferred to market-based exchange forms in capital intensive industries.

JOSKOW (1985)
Vertical integration between electric utilities and their input providers (coal mines increased because of specific investments operationalized as collocation decision of the mining and electricity generating operations.

LIBERMAN (1991)
Three main determinants of vertical integration are identified in an empirical analysis: (i) small-number situations ex-ante trigger vertical integration, (ii) highly transaction specific investments lead to ex-post haggling problems over quasi-rents and thereby make vertical integration more likely, (iii) the likelihood of vertical integration increases with input cost as a fraction of total production cost for a particular firm

---

Impact of IT on firm boundaries

MALONE ET AL (1987)
'Move-to-the-market hypothesis': the theoretical analysis shows an increase in market governance compared to hierarchical governance mechanisms mainly as a result of decreasing asset specificity

GURBAXANI/WHANG (1991)
Extend MALONE ET AL (1987): firm-internal transactions are also affected by information technology variables. The theoretical outcome of the impact of ICT on firm boundaries remains a function of the individual constellation of internal and external coordination costs

BAKOS (1992)
The effect of ICT on _intra_organizational coordination and production cost is more ambivalent than on _inter_organizational coordination

CLEMONS/ROW (1992)
'Move-to-the-middle hypothesis': investments in IT-based coordination between firms show low specificity and improve the ability of the firm to monitor compliance with arm's-length contracts. At the same time firms tend to rely on fewer business partners with whom the buyer has long-term relationships ('outsourcing cum fewer business partners')

BRYNJOLFSSON ET AL (1994)
The authors provide empirical support for the move-to-the-market hypothesis' by finding that IT leads to decreases in firm size

HOLLAND/LOCKETT (1997)	'Anything goes hypothesis'': no general rule exists in the relationship between IT and governance mode. The efficient mix of the two types of coordination mechanisms (markets and hierarchies) is determined on a case-to-case basis
GARICANO/KAPLAN (2000)	Empirical study of transaction data for an Internet-based car marketplace shows that IT-induced transaction cost reductions (transaction costs are defined as the sum of coordination and motivation cost): coordination cost are lowered while motivation costs for online transaction remained constant compared to physical transactions. The overall effect is a decrease in transaction costs
HITT (1998)	In an analysis of internal and external coordination cost using firm-level panel data, vertical integration and IT show a negative relationship on the firm level and on the industry level
SHIN (2002)	Decreases in vertical integration and weak increases in diversification can be attributed to the use of IT. R&D expenditure correlates positively with vertical integration

Institutional environment & firm boundaries

KUMAR ET AL (2001)	Analysis of the institutional determinants of variation in firm size: countries with a better institutional development have bigger firms because firms need external funds to grow
SCHIFFER/WEDER (2001)	The quality of governmental institutions is crucial for small firms. Small legal entities benefit from a sound institutional environment which leads to a negative relationship between firm boundaries and the institutional environment

Appendix II: ICT Variables

Information and Communication Technology Environment

(i)   ICTI (per capita)

Concept:

- Number of Internet hosts per capita per country

Measures:

- Computers connected to the Internet with an active Internet Protocol (IP) address
- Good proxy for ICT environment
- assumed to be negatively correlated with vertical integration by decreasing external/market coordination cost

Advantages and drawbacks:

- advantage: best proxy available because cross-country e-commerce data generally not available, host statistics is one of the best documented measure of cross-country ICT environment (the US started as one of the first countries to initiate national data collection for online purchases in March 2000). For recent years, figures on the number of secure servers are available that might be proxying the e-commerce aspect of the ICT environment more directly.
- advantage: international comparability of host statistics definitely higher than for figures featuring online purchases, also good proxy for development of other interorganizational forms of ICT
- drawback: URL / IP address is only prerequisite for e-commerce website. The result would be an overstatement of ICT development and thereby make its even more difficult to find significant results in the data. Finding a significant impact of ICT would suggest that the real effect might be even bigger.
- drawback: there is no guarantee that the company that registered a particular domain name is located in the country where it is registered.
  - o This problem is occurs only with generic top level domains (.com, .net, .org) and is unlikely to be a problem for national top level domains (.uk, .de, ...) Therefore, these top level domains are excluded from the analysis in order not to distort the validity of this measure. This proceeding follows OXLEY/YEUNG (2001)
- Reverse causality, i.e. the problem that vertical (dis-)integration might drive host count statistics seems to be not relevant here. ICT had the character of an exogenous shock on the economy. The reason is that ICT variables are, to a large extent, exogenous to firms. The number of Internet hosts / number of Internet users seems to depend more upon the institutional environment of a country than on firm decisions, see OXLEY/YEUNG (2001).

Source:

- International Telecommunication Union's (ITU) Yearbook of Statistics 2000 accessed via NYU's Euromonitor Database (internally available at NYU Stern's Ph.D. Research Resources website).
- Based on a semi-annual domain name survey, sponsored by the Internet Software Consortium (http://www.isc.org/)

(ii) ICTP (per capita)

Concept:
- Number of telephone lines per country per capita

Measures:
- proxy for communication environment

Source:
- ITU statistics via Euromonitor

(iii) ICTT (per capita)

Concept:
- Telecom Investments per capita per country

Measures:
- proxy for communication environment

Source:
- ITU statistics via Euromonitor

Appendix III: Definitions of Compustat Global Industrial/Commercial Items

- #1 Sales ..." Sales/Turnover (Net)": This item represents gross sales reduced by cash discounts, trade discounts, returned sales, excise taxes and value-added taxes and allowances for which credit is given to customers.

- #6 Raw Materials: This item represents the costs associated with the purchase or depletion of inventories/stocks.

- #14 Operating Income: This item represents the total income from normal business operations.

- #42 Staff Expense: This item represents direct payments to and indirect payments on behalf of, all employees.

- #52 Research and Development Expense: This item represents all costs incurred relating to development of new products or services.

- #89 Total Assets: This item represents the total value of assets reported on the Balance Sheet.

- #162 Number of Employees: This item represents the number of company workers as reported to shareholders.

Appendix IV: Variable Description

Variable	Measures	Source
Dependent Variables		
Vertical integration index	Value-added over total sales	(1)
Independent Variables		
Internet hosts per capita (ICTI)	Information technology penetration	(2)
Telephone lines per capita (ICTPPC)	Communication technology penetration	(2)
Telecommunication investment per capita (ICTTPC)	Communication technology penetration	(2)
EXP/GDP (exports as a proportion of GDP)	Degree of openness of economy (absence of cross-border integration)	(3)
GDP (Gross Domestic Product)	Market size	(3)
GDP_PC (Gross Domestic Product per capita)	Economic Development	(3)
LNINF (log annual rate of inflation)	Ability of a currency to represent stable value in contracting	(3)
R_D (Average R&D expenditure per country)	Country level R&D expenditure	(4)
POP (Population)	Market size	(4)
POLCON	Political environment	(5)
TAS_EMP (total assets per employee)	Capital intensity	(1)
SA_BY_AS (Total asset turnover)	Differences in asset management and efficiency	(1)
AS (Average total sales)	Firm Size	(1)
ATA (Average total assets)	Firm Size	(1)
LN_ANOE (Average number of employees, logged)	Firm Size	(1)
RDSAAV (R&D expenditure over sales)	Asset specificity, R&D investment over Sales	(1)
HIGH_CON (high ownership concentration)	Ownership concentration, dummy variable	(6)

(1) Compustat / Global Vantage, (2) International Telecommunication Union (via Euromonitor database), (3) International Financial Statistics / International Monetary Fund (via Euromonitor database) (4) National statistics (via Euromonitor database), (5) POLCON database, (6) LA PORTA Database

Appendix V: Sample Construction

The Compustat Global/Industrial Database is used to construct my vertical integration measure. The database was formerly known as Global Vantage (GV) and contains financial data on more than 12,000 companies in 65 countries around the world. Due to the creation of consistent financial data items the database allows meaningful cross-country comparisons.

First, I select all firms with SIC Code 2xxx –3xxx for 1990-2000 to reduce the industry bias. Then I eliminate from 50,874 firm years all firm years without values for 1990-2000 for the data items: #1 Sales, #6 Raw Materials, # 14 Operating Income, #42 Staff Expense, # 52 Research and Development Expense, # 89 Total Assets, #162 Number of Employees. This data selection routine allows a computation of the vertical integration measure for 559 firms. The cluster analysis is pursued with the 559 firms to identify differences in vertical integration in terms of the ICT environment these firms are located. The ICT environment is measured by creating three bins of country-years in terms of ICT penetration.

Subsequently, country-level data is created by aggregating firm level data. I omitted all firms without consistently reported data for the observed time period to avoid a bias from sample exit/entry of firms. This leads to a sample that contains aggregated data from 14 countries and 7 years.

Appendix VI: Digital Rights Management (DRM) Systems

According to SCHREIER ET AL (2001) there are three major models of DRM systems:

a) Prevention models: DRM systems that rely on encryption and access control in order to prevent file swapping. Copies to other consumers are prevented technically. Retailer collects revenues from consumers and pays IPR owner.

b) Advertisement-supported models: the music files that are exchanged are bundled with advertisement and promotion materials. The use of the music files is tracked by the DRM system via consumer responses to the advertisements. Certain proportion of advertisement revenues are channelled to IPR owner.

c) Marketplace models: music file exchange is controlled by making users that swap music files pay to a central clearinghouse for the use of the IPRs involved. Every time a music file is exchange the clearinghouse collects a fee and then compensates the IPR owner with these revenues.

Appendix VII: WPPT Member Countries

WPPT Member Countries	Sample Countries
Albania	Argentina*
Argentina*	Australia
Belarus	Austria
Bulgaria*	Brazil
Burkina Faso	Bulgaria*
Chile	Canada
Colombia	Chile
Costa Rica	Czech Republic
Croatia	Germany
Czech Republic	Denmark
Ecuador	Spain
El Salvador	France
Gabon	United Kingdom
Georgia	Greece
Guatemala	Hungary
Guinea	Indonesia
Honduras	Ireland
Hungary	Italy
Jamaica	Japan*
Japan*	Korea
Kyrgyzstan	Malaysia
Latvia	Mexico*
Lithuania	Netherlands
Mali	Norway
Mexico*	New Zealand
Mongolia	Poland
Nicaragua	Russia
Panama	United States of America*
Paraguay	South Africa
Peru	
Philippines	
Republic of Moldova	
Romania	
Saint Lucia	
Senegal	
Slovakia	
Slovenia	
Ukraine	
United States of America*	

* sample & WPPT member countries

Bibliography

ADELMAN, M.A. (1955), Concept and Statistical Measurement of Vertical Integration, in: *Business Concentration and Price Policy, A Conference of the Universities-National Bureau Committee For Economic Research*, Princeton, p. 281-322.

AGHION, P., DEWATRIPONT, M., REY, P. (1990), On Renegotiation Design, in: *European Economic Review*, 34(2/3), p. 322-329.

AGHION, P., DEWATRIPONT, M., REY, P. (1991), *Renegotiation Design with Unverifiable Information*, Mimeo.

ALBARRAN, A., DIMMICK, J. (1996), Concentration and Economics of Multiformity in the Communication Industries, in: *Journal of Media Economics*, 9(4), p. 45-51.

ALCHIAN, A.A., DEMSETZ, H. (1972), Production, Information Costs, and Economic Organization, in: *American Economic Review*, 62(5), p. 777-795.

ALCHIAN, A.A., WOODWARD, S. (1988), The Firm is Dead; Long Live the Firm. A Review of O. E. Williamson´s "The Economic Institutions of Capitalism", in: *Journal of Economic Literature*, 26(1), p. 65-79.

ALTMEPPEN, K.D. (1996), Märkte der Medienkommunikation, in: Altmeppen, K.D., (ed.), *Ökonomie der Medien und des Mediensystems*, Opladen, p. 251-272.

ANDERSON, E., WEITZ, B.A. (1986), Make or Buy Decisions: Vertical Integration and Marketing Productivity, in: *Sloan Management Review*, 27, p. 3-20.

ARMOUR, H.O., TEECE, D.J. (1980), Vertical integration and technological innovation, in: *Review of Economics and Statistics*, Vol. 62(3), p. 470-474.

ARROW, K.J. (1962), Economic Welfare and the Allocation of Resources for Inventions, in: Nelson, R.(ed.), *The Rate and Direction of Inventive Activity*, Princeton.

ARROW, K.J. (1969), The Organization of Economic Activity: Issues Pertinent to the Choice of Market versus Nonmarket Allocation, Analysis and Evaluation of Public Expenditures: *The PPB System, Joint Economic Committee, U.S. Congress*, p. 47-64.

ARROW, K.J. (1973), *Information and economic behavior*, Stockholm.

ARROW, K.J., DEBREU, G. (1954), Existence of an equilibrium for a competitive economy, in: *Econometrica*, 22(3), p. 265-290.

AUDRETSCH, D.B. (1995), The Innovation, Unemployment and Competitiveness Challenge in Germany, *CEPR Discussion Paper*, 1152.

BADARACCO, J. (1991), *The knowledge link: How firms compete through strategic alliances*, Boston.

BAKOS, Y. (1992), Information links and electronic marketplaces: The role of interorganizational information systems, in: *Journal of Management Information Systems*, 8(2) p. 31-52.

BAKOS, Y. (2001), The Emerging Landscape for Retail E-Commerce, in: *Journal of Economic Perspectives*, 15(1), p. 69-80.

BAKOS, Y., BRYNJOLFSSON, E. (1997), Organizational Partnerships and the virtual corporation, in: C. F. Kemerer (Ed.), *Information Technology and Industrial Competitiveness: How Information Technology Shapes Competition*, Amsterdam.

BALDWIN, T.F., McVOY, D.S., STEINFIELD, C. (1995), Convergence: Integrating Markets, in: *Telecommunications*, 32(10), p. 28-34.

BALTAGI, B.H. (1995), *Econometric Analysis of Panel Data*, Chichester.

BARKOULAS, J.T., BAUM, C.F., CHAKRABORTY, A. (2001), Waves and Persistence in Merger and Acquisition Activity, in: *Economics Letters*, 70(2), p. 237-243.

BARZEL, Y. (1982), Measurement Costs and the Organization of Markets, in: *Journal of Law and Economics*, 25(1), p. 27-48.

BAUER, S. (1997), *Auswirkungen der Informationstechnologie auf die vertikale Integration von Unternehmen*, Frankfurt am Main, zugl. Frankfurt (Oder), Univ., Diss.

BAUMOL, W.J., PANZAR, J., WILLIG, R. (1982), *Contestable Markets and the Theory of Industry Structure*, New York

BAUR, C. (1990), *Make-or-buy-Entscheidungen in einem Unternehmen der Automobilindustrie: Empirische Analyse und Gestaltung der Fertigungstiefe aus transaktionkostentheoretischer Sicht*, München, zugl. München, Univ., Diss,.

BECK, T., DEMIRGUEC-KUNT, A., MAKSIMOVIC, V. (2002), *Financial and legal constraints to firm growth: does size matter?*, World Bank Policy Research Working Paper 2905.

BECKER, G., MURPHY, K. (1992), The Division of Labor, Coordination Costs, and Knowledge, in: *Quarterly Journal of Economics*, 107(4), p. 1137-1160.

BENDER, C. (2001), A Gold Standard for the Internet? An Introductory Assessment, in: *EM - Electronic Markets*, 11(2), p. 121-125.

BENKLER, Y.(2002), Intellectual property and the organization of information production, in: *International Review of Law and Economics*, 22(1), p. 81-107.

BERNDT, E.R., MORRISON, C.J. (1991), Assessing the Productivity of Information Technology Equipment in U.S. Manufacturing Industries, *NBER Working Paper No. W3582*, January.

BESEN, S.M., RASKIND, L.J. (1991), An Introduction to the Law and Economics of Intellectual Property, in: *Journal of Economic Perspectives*, 5(1), p. 3-27.

BINMORE, K. (1992), *Fun and Games: A Text on Game Theory*, Heath.

BRADLACH, J.L., ECCLES, R.G. (1989), Price, Authority and Trust: From Ideal Types to Plural Forms, in: *American Review of Sociology*, 15, p. 97-118.

BRESNAHAN, T., BRYNJOLFSSON, E., HITT, L.M. (2002), Information Technology, Work Organization and the Demand for Skilled Labor: Firm-level Evidence, in: *Quarterly Journal of Economics*, 117(1), p. 339-376.

BROUSSEAU, E. (1999), *The Governance of Transaction by Commercial Intermediaries: An Analysis of the Re-engineering of Intermediation by Electronic Commerce*, Paper presented at the 3rd Conference of the International Society for New Institutional Economics, September 16th-18th, 1999, Washington DC, USA.

BROUSSEAU, E., FARES, M. (1998), Incomplete Contracts and Governance Structures: Are Incomplete Contract Theory and New Institutional Economics Substitutes or Complements?, in: Menard, C. (2000), *Institutions, Contracts, and Organizations: Perspectives from New Institutional Economics*, Cheltenham.

BROWN, J.R., GOOLSBEE, A. (2000), Does the Internet Make Markets More Competitive?, *NBER Working Paper No. W7996*, November.

BRYNJOLFSSON, E., HITT, L., YANG, S. (2000), *Intangible Assets: How the Interaction of Information Technology and Organizational Structure Affects Stock Market Valuations*, MIT Working Paper.

BRYNJOLFSSON, E., MALONE, T. W., GURBAXANI, V., KAMBIL, A. (1994). "Does Information Technology Lead to Smaller Firms?" *Management Science*, 40(12), p. 1628-1644.

BUCHANAN, J.M. (1965), An Economic Theory of Clubs, in: *Economica*, 32(1), p. 1-14.

BUCHANAN, J.M. (1992), Economics in the Post-Socialist Century, in: Hey, J. D. (ed.), *The Future of Economics*, Oxford.

BUCKLEY, P.J., CASSON, M. (1991), *The future of the multinational enterprise*, London.

BUZELL, R.D., GALE, B.T. (1989), *Das Pims-Programm, Strategien und Unternehmenserfolg*, Wiesbaden.

CALVET, A.L. (1981), A synthesis of foreign direct investment theories and theories of the multinational firm, in: *Journal of International Business Studies*, 12(1), p. 43-59.

CARLSSON, B. (1988), *The Evolution of Manufacturing Technology and its Impact on Industrial Structure: An International Study,* The Industrial Institute for Economic and Social Research, Stockholm.

CARTER, B. (1998), The Thursday night massacre. *The New York Times Magazine,* September 20th, p. 65-68.

CASADESUS-MASANELL, R., SPULBER, D.F. (2000), The Fable of Fisher Body, in: *Journal of Law and Economics*, 43(1), p. 67-104.

CASSON, M. (1987), *The firm and the market*, Oxford.

CAVES, R.E., BRADBURD, R.M. (1988), The empirical determinants of vertical integration, in: *Journal of Economic Behavior and Organization*, 9(3), p. 265-279

CHANDLER, A. (1977), The Visible Hand, Cambridge, MA.

CLAESSENS, S., DJANKOV, S., FAN, J., LANG, L. (1999), *The Benefits and Costs of Internal Markets, Evidence from Asia's Financial Crisis*, World Bank manuscript.

CLEMONS, E.K., REDDI, S.P., ROW, M. (1993), The impact of information technology on the organization of economic activity: the 'move to the middle' hypothesis, in: *Journal of Management Information Systems*, 10(2), p. 9-35.

CLEMONS, E.K., ROW, M.C. (1992), Information technology and industrial cooperation: the changing economics of coordination and ownership, in: *Journal of Management Information Systems*, 9(2), p. 9-28.

COASE, R. (1937), The Nature of the Firm, in: *Economica*, 4(16), p. 386-405.

COASE, R. (1960), The Problem of Social Cost, in: *Journal of Law and Economics*, 3(1), p. 1-44.

COASE, R. (1992), The Institutional Structure of Production: The 1991 Alfred Nobel Memorial Prize Lecture in Economic Sciences, in: *American Economic Review*, 82(4), p. 713-719.

COASE, R. (2002), Why Economics Will Change, Remarks at the University of Missouri, Columbia, Missouri, April 4, 2002, in: *International Society for New Institutional Economics Newsletter*, Summer 2002, 4(1), p. 1-7.

COLLIS, D.J., BANE, P.W., BRADLEY, S.P. (1997), *Winners and Losers: Industry Structure in the Age of Digital Convergence*, Boston.

COMMONS, J. (1934), *Institutional Economics: Its place in Political Economy*, Madison.

CUSUMANO, M.A. , TAKEISHI, A. (1991), Supplier Relations and Management: A Survey of Japanese, Japanese-Transplant, and U.S. Auto Plants, in: *Strategic Management Journal*, 12(8), p. 563-588.

DAVENPORT, T.H. (1993), *Process Innovation – Reengineering Work Through Information Technology*, Boston.

DAVIS, L.E., NORTH, D.C. (1971), *Institutional Change and American Economic Growth*, Cambridge.

DAY, J.D., WENDLER, J.C. (1998), The New Economics of Organization, in: *The McKinsey Quarterly*, 1, p. 4-17

DOIG, S.J., RITTER, R.C., SPECKHALS, K., WOOLSON, D. (2001), Has outsourcing gone too far?, in: *The McKinsey Quarterly*, 4, p. 26.

DYER, J.H., SINGH, H. (1998), The relational view: cooperative strategy and sources of interorganizational competitive advantage, in: *Academy of Management Review*, 23(4), p. 660-679.

EBERS, M. (1994), Interorganisationale Informationssysteme - Eine transaktionskosten-theoretische Betrachtung, in: Sydow, J., Windeler, A. (eds.), *Management interorganisationaler Beziehungen*, Opladen, p. 22-48.

ECONOMIDES, N. (1996), The Economics of Networks, in: *International Journal of Industrial Organization*, 14(6), p. 673-699.

ELLRAM, L.M. (1991), Supply Chain Management: The Industrial Organization Perspective, in: *International Journal of Physical Distribution and Logistics Management*, 21(1), p. 13-21.

EVANS, P., WURSTER, T. (1999), *Blown to Bits: How the New Economics of Information Transforms Strategy*, Cambridge, MA.

FEENSTRA, R.C. (1998), Integration of Trade and Disintegration of Production in the Global Economy, in: *Journal of Economic Perspectives*, 12(4), p. 31-50.

FEENSTRA, R.C., HANSON, G.H. (1997), Foreign Direct Investment and Relative Wages: Evidence from Mexico's Maquiladoras, in: *Journal of International Economics*, 42(3/4), p. 371-393.

FRANKS, J., MAYER, C. (1994), *The ownership and control of German corporations*, Mimeo, London Business School.

FRITSCH, M., WEIN, T., EWERS, H.-J. (1996), *Marktversagen und Wirtschaftspolitik: mikroökonomische Grundlagen staatlichen Handelns*, Munich.

FURUBOTN, E.G., RICHTER, R. (1989), *Institutions and Economic Theory, The Contribution of the New Institutional Economics*, Ann Arbor.

GALLAGHER, T. (2001), Copyright Compulsory Licensing and Incentives, *Oxford Intellectual Property Research Center Working Paper Series*, 2, May.

GALBRAITH, J. (1977), *Organizational Design*, Reading.

GARDINI, F. (2002), *The forward vertical integration of movie studios into TV networks: a comparison between theoretical frameworks*; Conference Paper, 5th World Media Economics Conference, Turku, Finland, May 2002.

GARICANO, L., KAPLAN, S.N. (2000), The Effects of Business-to-Business E-Commerce on Transaction Costs, *NBER Working Paper No. W8017*, November.

GEIHS, K. (1995), *Client / Server-Systeme: Grundlagen und Architekturen*, Bonn

GERSCHENKRON, A. (1962), *Economic Backwardness in Historical Perspective*, reprinted in Economic Backwardness in Historical Perspective, Cambridge, MA.

GHOSHAL, S., MORAN, P. (1996), Bad for practice: A critique of the transaction cost theory, in: *Academy of Management Review*, 21(1), p. 13-47.

GILBERT, R., SHAPIRO, C. (1990), Optimal Patent Length and Breadth, in: *Rand Journal of Economics*, 21(1), p. 106-112.

GILSON, R.J., ROE, M.J. (1993), Understanding the Japanese Keiretsu: Overlaps Between Corporate Governance and Industrial Organization, in: *The Yale Law Journal*, 102(4), p. 871-906.

GINARTE, J.C., PARK, W.G. (1997), Determinants of patent rights: A cross-national study, in: *Research Policy*, 26(3), p. 283-301.

GLOBERMAN, S. (1980), Markets, hierarchies and innovation, in: *Journal of Economic Issues*, 14(4), p. 977-998.

GRANOVETTER, M. (1985), Economic Action and Social Structure: The Problem of Embeddedness, in: *American Journal of Sociology*, 91(3), p. 481-510.

GREENE, W. (2000), *Econometric Analysis*, 4th ed., Upper Saddle River.

GREENSTEIN, S., KHANNA, T. (1997), What does industry convergence mean?, in: Yoffie, D.B. (Ed.), *Competing in the age of digital convergence*, Boston, p. 201-226

GRILICHES, Z.(1984), R&D and productivity growth at the firm level, in: Griliches, Z. (ed.), *Research & Development, Patents and Productivity*, Chicago.

GROEMLING, M., LICHTBLAU, K., WEBER, A. (1998), *Industrie und Dienstleistungen im Zeitalter der Globalisierung*, Köln.

GROSSMAN, S., HART, O. (1986), The Costs and Benefits of Ownership: A Theory of Vertical and Lateral Integration, in: *Journal of Political Economy*, 94(4), p. 691-719.

GURBAXANI, V., WHANG, S. (1991), The Impact of Information Systems on Organizations and Markets, in: *Communications of the Association for Computing Machinery*, 34(1), p. 59-73.

HALLER, A., STOLOWY, H. (1998), Value Added in Financial Accounting: A Comparative Study of Germany and France, in: *Advances in International Accounting*, 11, p. 23-51.

HARM, C. (1996), *Communication Costs and Authority: An Economic Theory of Management*, Working Paper, Copenhagen Business School, Nov.

HARM, C. (2001), *A Plea for more Politics in the International Business Research Agenda*, Working Paper, University of Münster, March.

HART, O. (1987), Incomplete Contracts, in: Eatwell, J., Milgate, M., Newman, P. (eds.), *The New Palgrave: A Dictionary of Economics*, 2, London, p. 752-759.

HART, O. (1995), *Firms, Contracts, and Financial Structure, Clarendon Lectures in Economics*, Oxford.

HART, O., HOLMSTRØM, B.R. (1987), The Theory of Contracts, in: Bewley, T. (ed.), *Advances in Economic Theory*, Cambridge, p. 71-155.

HART, O., MOORE, J. (1988), Incomplete Contracts and Renegotiation, in: *Econometrica*, 56(4), p. 755-785.

HASENKAMP, U., KIRN, S., SYRING, M. (1994), *CSCW - Computer Supported Cooperative Work*, Bonn.

HAUSMAN, J.A. (1978), Specification Tests in Econometrics, in: *Econometrica*, 46(6), p. 1251-1271.

HAYEK, F.A. (1945), The Use of Knowledge in Society, in: *American Economic Review*, 35(4), September, p. 519-530.

HAYEK, F.A. (1969), *Freiburger Studien - Gesammelte Aufsätze*, Tübingen.

HENISZ, W., DELIOS, A. (2002), Learning About the Institutional Environment, in: INGRAM, P., SILVERMAN, B. (eds.), *The New Institutionalism in Strategic Management,* 19, forthcoming.

HENISZ, W. (2002), The Institutional Environment for Infrastructure Investment, in: *Industrial and Corporate Change*, 11(2), p. 355-389.

HENNART, J.F. (1988), Upstream vertical integration in the Aluminium and Tin Industries, in: *Journal of Economic Behavior and Organisation*, 9(3), p. 281-299.

HITT, L.M. (1998), *Information Technology and Firm Boundaries: Evidence from Panel Data*, Working Paper, University of Pennsylvania, The Wharton School, August 1998.

HOFSTEDE, G. (1980), *Culture's consequences: International differences in work-related values*, Beverly Hills.

HOLLAND, C.P., LOCKETT, A.G. (1997), Mixed Mode Network Structures: The Strategic Use of Electronic Communication by Organizations, in: *Organization Science*, 8(5), p. 475-488.

HOLMSTRØM, B., ROBERTS, J, (1998) The Boundaries of the Firm Revisited, in: *Journal of Economic Perspectives*, 12(4), p. 73-94.

HSIAO, C. (1986), *Analysis of Panel Data*, Cambridge.

HUMMELS, D., RAPOPORT, D., YI, K.-M. (1998), Vertical Specialization and the Changing Nature of World Trade, in: *FRBNY Economic Policy Review*, 4(2), p. 79-99.

IFPI (2001), *The Recording Industry in Numbers*, edited by the International Federation of the Phonographic Industry, London.

IFPI (2002), *The Recording Industry in Numbers,* edited by the International Federation of the Phonographic Industry, London.

IFPI (2002), *Music Piracy Report 2002*, edited by the International Federation of the Phonographic Industry, London.

INTERNATIONAL DATA CORPORATION (2000), *The Future of the Music Industry: MP3, DVD-Audio, and More.*

JENSEN, M.C., MECKLING, W.H. (1976), Theory of the Firm: Managerial Behavior, Agency Costs and Ownership Structure, in: *Journal of Financial Economics*, 3(4), p. 305-360.

JOBSON, J.D. (1992a), *Applied Multivariate Data Analysis, Vol. I: Regression and Experimental Design*, New York.

JOBSON, J.D. (1992b), *Applied Multivariate Data Analysis, Vol. II: Categorical and Multivariate Methods*, New York.

JOHNSON, W.R. (1985), The Economics of Copying, in: *Journal of Political Economy*, 93(1), p. 158-174.

JOSKOW, P.L. (1985), Vertical Integration and long-term contracts: The case of coal burning electric generating plants, in: *Journal of Law, Economics, and Organization*, 1(1), p. 33-80.

JOSKOW, P.L. (1988), Asset specificity and the structure of vertical relationships: Empirical evidence, in: Journal of Law, Economics and Organization, 4(1), p. 95-117.

JUDGE, G.G., GRIFFITHS, W.E., HILL, R.C., LUTKEPOHL, H., LEE, T.C. (1985), The Theory and Practice of Econometrics, New York.

JUPITER RESEARCH (2001), *Music Forecast 2001*, 3, p. 1.

KAMBIL, A. (1991), Information technology and vertical integration: Evidence from the manufacturing sector, in: Calvert-Guerin, M., Wildman, S. (eds.), *Electronics services networks: A business and public policy challenge*, New York, p. 22-38.

KANE, E.J. (1981), Accelerating Inflation, Technological Innovation, and the Decreasing Effectiveness of Banking Regulation, in: *Journal of Finance*, 36(2), p. 355-67.

KAPLAN, S., MINTON, B. (1994), Appointments of outsiders to Japanese boards: determinants and implications for manager, in: *Journal of Financial Economics*, 36(2), p. 225-257.

KATZ, M., SHAPIRO, C. (1994), Systems Competition and Network Effects, in: *Journal of Economic Perspectives*, 8(2), p. 93-115.

KAUFMANN, F. (1966), Data Systems that Cross Company Boundaries, in: *Harvard Business Review*, 44(1), p. 141-155.

KENNEDY, P. (1998), *A Guide to Econometrics*, 4th ed., Cambridge, MA.

KERKVLIET, J. (1991), Efficiency and vertical integration: The case of mine mouth electric generating plants, in: *The Journal of Industrial Economics*, 39(5), p. 467-481.

KIRSCH, G. (1997), *Neue Politische Ökonomie*, 4th ed., Düsseldorf.

KLEIN, B., CRAWFORD, R.G., ALCHIAN, A.A. (1978), Vertical integration, appropriable rents, and the competitive contracting process, in: *Journal of Law and Economics*, 21(2), p. 21(2), p. 297-326.

KLEIN, S. (1996), *Interorganisationssysteme und Unternehmensnetzwerke:Wechselwirkungen zwischen organisatorischer und informationstechnischer Entwicklung*, Wiesbaden.

KLEIN, S. (1997), Zur Rolle moderner Informations- und Kommunikationstechnik, in: Müller-Stewens (ed.), *Virtualisierung von Organisationen, Entwicklungstendenzen im Management*, Bd. 16, Stuttgart.

KOHLI, R., SHERER, S. (2002), Measuring Payoff of Information Technology Investments: Research Issues and Guidelines, in: *Communications of the Association for Information Systems*, 9(14), p. 241-268.

KOZICKI, S. (1997), The productivity growth slowdown: Diverging trends in the manufacturing and service sectors, in: *The Federal Reserve Bank of Kansas City Economic Review*; 82(1), p. 31-46.

KRUGMAN, P. (1995), Growing World Trade: Causes and Consequences, in: *Brookings Papers on Economic Activity*, 26(1), p. 327-62.

KUMAR, K.B., RAJAN, R.G., ZINGALES, L. (2001), What determines firm size?, *NBER Working Paper W7208*, July 1999, this version: mimeo, Graduate School of Business, University of Chicago, March 2001.

LA PORTA, R., LOPEZ-DE-SILANES, F., SHLEIFER, A., VISHNY, R. (1997a), Trust in Large Organizations, in: *American Economic Review*, 87(2), p. 333-338.

LA PORTA, R., LOPEZ-DE-SILANES, F., SHLEIFER, A., VISHNY, R. (1997b), Legal Determinants of External Finance, in: *Journal of Finance*, 52(3), p. 1131-1150.

LA PORTA, R., LOPEZ-DE-SILANES, F., SHLEIFER, A., VISHNY, R. (1998), Law and Finance, in: *Journal of Political Economy*, 106(6), p. 1113-1155.

LAFFER, A.B. (1969), Vertical Integration by Corporations 1929-1965, in: *The Review of Economics and Statistics*, 51(1), p. 91-93.

LANDES, W.M., POSNER, R.A. (1989), An Economic Analysis of Copyright Law, in: *Journal of Legal Studies*, 18, p. 325-363.

LAWSON, A.M., TESKE, D.A. (1994), Benchmark Input Output Accounts for the U.S. Economy, in: *Survey of Current Business*, 74(4), p. 73-115.

LEHMAN BROTHERS (2001), *Research Report: A Celestial Jukebox*.

LEHMANN, E., WEIGAND, J. (2000), Does the Governed Corporation Perform Better? Governance Structures and Corporate Performance in Germany, in: *European Finance Review*, 4(2), p. 157–195.

LEHMANN, M.R. (1954), *Leistungsmessung durch Wertschöpfungsrechnung*, Essen.

LEVENSTEIN, M.C. (2002), Vertical Integration, in: Mokyr, J. (ed.), *Oxford Encyclopedia of Economic History*, Oxford, forthcoming.

LEVINTHAL, D.A., FICHMAN, M. (1988), Dynamics of interorganizational attachments: auditor-client relationships, in: *Administrative Science Quarterly*, 33(3), p. 345-360.

LEVY, D.T. (1985), The transaction cost approach to vertical integration: An empirical investigation, in: *The Review of Economics and Statistics*, 67(3), p. 438-445.

LIEBERMAN, M.B. (1991), Determinants of Vertical Integration: An Empirical Test, in: *Journal of Industrial Economics*, 39(5), p. 451-466.

LIEBOWITZ, S. (2002), *Rethinking the Network Economy*, New York.

LIEBOWITZ, S., MARGOLIS, S.E. (1990), The Fable of the Keys, in: *Journal of Law and Economics*, 33(1), p. 1-26.

LOEFFLER, E. (1991), *Der Konzern als Finanzintermediär*, Wiesbaden.

LUNN, J. (1985), The Roles of Property Rights and Market Power in Appropriating Innovative Output, in: *The Journal of Legal Studies*, 14(4), p. 423-433.

MACDONALD, J.M. (1985), Market exchange or vertical integration: An empirical analysis, in: *Review of Economics and Statistics*, 67(2), p. 327-331.

MACKIE-MASON, J. (2000), An AOL/Time Warner Merger Will Harm Competition in Internet Online Services, Report to the U.S. Federal Trade Commission, October.

MADDIGAN, R. (1981), The Measurement of Vertical Integration, in: *Review of Economics and Statistics*, 63(3), p. 328-335.

MALONE, T.W., BENJAMIN, R.I., YATES, J. (1987), Electronic markets and electronic hierarchies: effects of information technology on market structure and corporate strategies, in: *Communications of the Association for Computing Machinery*, 30(6), p. 484-497.

MARSHALL, A. (1952), *Principles of Economics*, 8th ed., London.

MASTEN, S.E. (1984), The organization of production: evidence from the aerospace industury, in: *Journal of Law and Economics*, 27(2), p. 403-417.

MASUD, S. (1998), *Telecom merger mania: New strategies, players, and media, information & Communication*, Thousand Oaks.

MATJE, A. (1994), Anmerkungen zur wertschöpfungsorientierten Messung vertikaler Integration aus betriebswirtschaftlicher Sicht, in: Seicht, G. (ed.), *Kostenrechnung und Kostenmanagement, Buchhaltung und Bilanzierung, Konzernrechnungslegung, Krisenmanagement und Gläubigerschutz, Cash-flow und Kapitalflussrechnung, Öko-Controlling*, Wien, p. 303-334.

MCKINSEY GLOBAL INSTITUTE (2001), *US Productivity Growth 1995-2000, Understanding the contribution of Information Technology relative to other factors*.

MCLAREN, J. (2000), Globalization and Vertical Structure, in: *American Economic Review* 90(5), December, p. 1239-1254.

MENARD, C. (1996), On Clusters, Hybrids and other Strange Forms. The Case of the French Poultry Industry, in: *Journal of Institutional and Theoretical Economics*, 152(1), p.154-183.

MENARD, C. (2002), *The Economics of Hybrid Organizations*, Presidential Address, 6th Conference of the International Society for New Institutional Economics, September 27th-29th, 2002, Boston.

MILGROM, P., ROBERTS, J. (1992), *Economics, Organization and Management*, Englewood Cliffs.

MONTEVERDE, K., TEECE, D. (1982), Supplier switching costs and vertical integration in the automobile industry, in: *Bell Journal of Economics*,13(1), p. 206-213.

MOORE, J. (1992), Implementation in Environments with Complete Information, in: Laffont, J.J. (ed.), *Advances in Economic Theory*, Cambridge, p. 182-282.

MORCK, R., YEUNG, B. (1991), Why Investors Value Multinationality, in: *Journal of Business*, 64(2), p. 165-187.

MUSGRAVE, R.A. (1959), *The Theory of Public Finance*, New York.

MUSGRAVE, R.A., MUSGRAVE, P.B. (1989), *Public finance in theory and practice*, New York.

NEUBURGER, R. (1994), *Electronic Data Interchange – Einsatzmöglichkeiten und ökonomische Auswirkungen*, Wiesbaden.

NOOTEBOOM, B. (1996), Trust, opportunism and governance: a process and control model, in: *Organization Studies*, 17(6), p. 985-1010.

NORDHAUS, W.D. (1969), *Invention, Growth and Welfare: A Theoretical Treatment of Technological Change*, Cambridge, MA.

NORTH, D.C., WALLIS, J.J. (1994), Integrating Institutional Change and Technical Change in Economic History: A Transaction Cost Approach, in: *Journal of Institutional and Theoretical Economics*, 150(4), p. 609-624.

OESTERLE, H., FLEISCH, E., ALT, R. (2000), *Business Networking – Shaping Enterprise Relationship on the Internet*, Berlin.

OUCHI, W.G. (1980), Markets, bureaucracies and clans, in: *Administrative Science Quarterly*, 25(3), p. 129-141.

OUCHI, W.G., WILLIAMSON, O.E. (1981), The markets and hierarchies perspective: origins, implications, prospects, in: Van den Ven, A., Joyce, W.F. (eds.), *Assessing Organizational Design and Performance*, New York, p. 347-370.

OXLEY, J. (1999), Institutional environment and the mechanisms of governance: The impact of intellectual property protection on the structure of inter-firm alliances, in: *Journal of Economic Behavior and Organization*, 38(3), p.283-309.

OXLEY, J., YEUNG, B. (2001), E-Commerce Readiness – Institutional Environment and International Competitiveness, in: *Journal of International Business Studies*, 32(4), p. 705-723.

PALERMO, A., MCCREADY, S. (1992), Workflow Software: A Primer, in: Coleman, D. (ed.), *Groupware '92*, San Mateo, p. 155-159.

PARSONS, T., SMELSER, N.J. (1956), *Economy and Society*, New York.

PAY, D. (1989), *Die Organisation von Innovationen*, Wiesbaden.

PFAFFMANN, E. (1998), Ein Modell der vertikalen Keiretsu – Eine ökonomische Analyse der Wettbewerbsvorteile und Ranghierarchie für Subkontraktoren am Beispiel der Automobilindustrie, in: *Die Betriebswirtschaft*, 58(4), p. 451-466.

PICOT, A. (1982), Transaktionskostenansatz in der Organisationstheorie: Stand der Diskussion und Aussagewert, in: *Die Betriebswirtschaft*, 42(2), p. 267-284.

PICOT, A. (1991), Ein neuer Ansatz zur Gestaltung der Leistungstiefe, in: *Zeitschrift für betriebswirtschaftliche Forschung*, 43 (4), p. 336-357.

PICOT, A., REICHWALD, R., WIGAND, R. (2001), *Die grenzenlose Unternehmung – Information, Organisation und Management*, Wiesbaden, 4th ed. English translation: WIGAND, R., PICOT, A., REICHWALD, R. (1997), Information, Organization and Management: Expanding Markets and Corporate Boundaries, Chichester.

PICOT, A., RIPPERGER, T., WOLFF, B. (1996), The Fading Boundaries of the Firm, in: *Journal of Institutional and Theoretical Economics*, 152(1), p. 65-79.

PIGOU, A.C. (1938), *The Economics of Welfare*, 4th ed., London.

PIORE, M., SABEL, C. (1984), *The Second Industrial Divide*, New York.

PORTER, A.M. (1999), Outsourcing gains popularity, *Purchasing Survey*, March 11th.

PRICEWATERHOUSECOOPERS (2001), *The Opacity Index*, January.

RAJAN, R., ZINGALES, L. (1998a), Power in a Theory of the Firm, in: *Quarterly Journal of Economics*, 113(2), p. 387-432.

RAJAN, R., ZINGALES, L. (1998b), Financial Dependence and Growth, in: *American Economic Review*, 88(3), p. 559-586.

RAJAN, R., ZINGALES, L. (2000), The Governance of the New Corporation, in: Vives, X. (ed.), *Corporate Governance*, Cambridge, p. 201-229.

RAJAN, R., ZINGALES, L. (2001), The Firm as a Dedicated Hierarchy: A Theory of the Origins and Growth of Firms, in: *Quarterly Journal of Economics*, 116(3), p. 805-852.

RICHARDSON, G.B. (1972), The Organization of Industry, in: *Economic Journal*, 82(327), p. 883-896.

RIEMER, K., KLEIN, S., SELZ, D. (2001), Classification of dynamic organizational forms and coordination roles, in: Stanford-Smith, B., Chiozza, E. (eds.), *E-work and E-commerce*

(Proceedings of the e2001 Conference on E-work and E-business, Venice 2001), IOS Press, Amsterdam, p. 825-831.

RUGMAN, A.M. (1986), New theories of the multinational enterprise-An assessment of internationalization theory, in: *Bulletin of Economic Research*, 38(2), p. 1010-1018.

SAALBACH, H.P. (1996), *Das Konzept der Transaktionskosten in der Neuen Institutionenökonomik*, Marburg.

SAMUELSON, P. (1954), The pure theory of public expenditure, in: *Review of Economics and Statistics*, 36(6), p. 387-389.

SCHERER, F.M. (1972), Nordhaus' Theory of Optimal Patent Life: A geometric Reinterpretation, in: *American Economic Review*, 62(3), p. 422-427.

SCHIFFER, M., WEDER, B. (2001), *Firm Size and the Business Environment: Worldwide Survey Results*, IFC Discussion Paper, No. 43, also: Proceedings of the 6th Conference of the International Society for New Institutional Economics Conference, September 27th-29th, 2002, Boston.

SCHMALENSEE, R., WILLIG, R. (1989), *Handbook of Industrial Organization, Vol. 1*, New York.

SCHREIER, E., BERNOFF, J., SORLEY, J., GERSON, M. (2000), *Content Out of Control*, The Forrester Report, Sept.

SCHUMANN, J. (1992), *Grundzüge der mikroökonomischen Theorie*, 6th ed., Berlin.

SCHUMPETER, J.A. (1942), *Capitalism, Socialism, and Democracy*, New York.

SCOTCHMER, S. (1991), Standing on the Shoulders of Giants: Cumulative Research and the Patent Law, in: *Journal of Economic Perspectives*, 5 (1), p. 29-41.

SHAPIRO, C., VARIAN, H.R. (1999), *Information Rules: A Strategic Guide to the Network Economy*, Boston.

SHAVER, M., FLYER, F. (2000), Agglomeration economies, firm heterogeneity, and foreign direct investment in the United States, in: *Strategic Management Journal*, 21(12), p. 1175-1193.

SHELANSKI, H.A., KLEIN, P.G. (1995), Empirical Research in Transaction Cost Economics: A Review and Assessment, in: *Journal of Law, Economics, and Organization*, 11(2), p. 335-361.

SHERMAN, R.J. (1998), Collaborative planning, forecasting & replenishment (CPFR): Realizing the promise of efficient consumer response through collaborative technology, in: *Journal of Marketing Theory and Practice*, 6(4), p. 6-9.

SHIN, N. (2002), Empirical Analysis of the impact of information technology on vertical integration, in: *International Journal of Services, Technology & Management*, forthcoming.

SIMON, H.A. (1957), *Administrative Behavior: A study of decision-making processes in administrative organization*, 2nd ed., New York.

SIMON, H.A. (1978), Rationality as Process and as Product of Thought, in: *American Economic Review, Papers and Proceedings*, 68(2), p. 1-16.

SOLOW, R.S. (1987), We'd Better Watch Out, in: *New York Times Book Review*.

SPENGLER, J. (1950), Vertical integration and anti-trust policy, in: *Journal of Political Economy*, 58(4), p. 347-352.

SPILLER, P.T. (1985), On vertical mergers, in: *Journal of Law, Economics, and Organization*, 1(2), p. 285-312.

STAATZ, J.M. (1983), The Cooperative as a Coalition: A Game-Theoretic Approach, in: *American Journal of Agricultural Economics*, 65(5), p. 1084-1089.

STERN, L.W., CRAIG, S.C. (1971), Interorganizational Data Systems – The Computer and Distribution, in: *Journal of Retailing*, 47(2), p. 73-91.

STIGLER, G.J. (1951), The division of labour is limited by the extent of the market, in: The *Journal of Political Economy*, 59(3), p. 185-193.

STIGLER, G.J. (1961), The Economics of Information, in: *Journal of Political Economy*, 69(3), p. 213-225.

STUDEMUND, A.H. (1997), *Using Econometrics – A Practical Guide*, 3rd ed., Reading.

TANDON, P. (1982), Optimal Patents with Compulsory Licensing, in: *Journal of Political Economy*, 90(3), p. 470-486.

TAPSCOTT, D. (1995), *Digital Economy. Promise and Peril in the Age of Networked Intelligence*, New York.

TEECE, D.J. (1986a), Transaction cost economics and the multinational enterprise, in: *Journal of Economic Behavior and Organization*, 7(1), p. 21-45.

TEECE, D.J. (1986b), Profiting from Technological Innovation, in: *Research Policy*, 15(6), p. 285-305.

THE ECONOMIST (2000a), *Have factory, will travel*, Feb 10th.

THE ECONOMIST (2000b), *The Shape of the New E-Company*, Nov 9th.

THE ECONOMIST (2000c), *Catch up if you can*, E-Commerce Survey, Sep 21st.

THE ECONOMIST (2000d), *Falling through the net?*, E-Commerce Survey, Sep 21st.

THE ECONOMIST (2001a), *E-strategy brief: Siemens*, June 2nd.

THE ECONOMIST (2001b), *Will the corporation survive?*, Survey: The Near Future, Nov 1st.

THE ECONOMIST (2001c), *The Great Convergence Gamble*, Dec 7th.

THE ECONOMIST (2002a), *Tangled Webs*, May 23rd.

THE ECONOMIST (2002b), *What is the point?*, May 23rd.

THE ECONOMIST (2002c), *Napster R.I.P*, Sept 5th.

TIROLE, J. (1992), *The Theory of Industrial Organization*, Cambridge, MA, 5th ed.

TIROLE, J. (1994), *Incomplete Contracts: Where do we stand?*, Walras-Bowley Lecture to the Econometric Society, Quebec City.

TRYON, R.C. (1939), *Cluster Analysis: Correlation Profile and Orthometric (Factor Analysis for the Isolation of Unities in Mind and Personality)*, Ann Arbor.

TSENG, K.F., LITMAN, B. (1998), The impact of the Telecommunications Act of 1996 on the merger of RBOCs and MSOs: Case study: The Merger of US West and Continental Cablevision, in: *Journal of Media Economics*, 11(3), p. 47-64.

TUCKER, I.B., WILDER, R.P. (1977), Trends in vertical integration in the US manufacturing sector, in: *Journal of Industrial Economics*, 26(1), p. 81-94.

UTTERBACK, J. M., SUÁREZ, F. F. (1993), Innovation, Competition, and Industry Structure, in: *Research Policy*, 22(1), p. 1-22.

UZZI, B. (1997), Social structure and competition in interfirm networks: The paradox of embeddedness, in: *Administrative Science Quarterly*, 42(1), p. 35-67.

VERKEHRSBRIEF (2001), Automobilbau - Bonanza für Module, 15 June 2001.

VOGEL, H. (2001), *Entertainment Industry Economics*, Cambridge, 5th ed.

VOLLMUTH, H.J. (1998), *Kennzahlen*, Planegg.

WALKER, J., FERGUSON, D. (1998), *The broadcast television industry*, Needham Heights.

WALTER, I. (1990), *The Secret Money Market, Inside the Dark World of Tax Evasion, Financial Fraud, Insider Trading, Money Laundering, and Capital Flight*, New York.

WIEGRAN, G. (1993), Transaktionsksotenanalyse in der Personalwirtschaft, in: *Zeitschrift für Organisation*, 62(4), p. 264-267.

WILLIAMSON, O.E. (1975), *Markets and hierarchies: Analysis of Antitrust Implications*, New York.

WILLIAMSON, O.E. (1981a), The modern Corporation: Origin, Evolution, Attributes, in: *Journal of Economic Literature*, 19(4), p. 1537-1568.

WILLIAMSON, O.E. (1981b), The Economics of Organization: The Transaction Cost Approach, in: *American Journal of Sociology*, 87(3), p.548-577.

WILLIAMSON, O.E. (1985), *The Economic Institutions of Capitalism*, New York.

WILLIAMSON, O.E. (1987), *Antitrust Economics: Mergers, Contracting, and Strategic Behavior*, Oxford.

WILLIAMSON, O.E. (1991), Comparative Economic Organization: The Analysis of Discrete Structural Alternatives, in: *Administrative Science Quarterly*, 36(2), p. 269-296.

WILLIAMSON, O.E. (1996), *The Mechanisms of Governance*, New York.

WIRTZ, B.W. (2001), *Medien- und Internetmanagement*, Wiesbaden.

WU, Y., ZHANG, J. (2001), The Effects of Inflation on the Number of Firms and Firm Size, in: *Journal of Money, Credit, and Banking*, 33(2), Part 1, p. 251-271.

YU, B.T. (1981), Potential Competition and Contracting in Innovation, in: *Journal of Law and Economics*, 24(2), p. 215-238.

ZAEPFEL, G. (1989), *Strategisches Produktionsmanagement*, Berlin, New York.

ZECKHAUSER, R., POUND, P. (1990), Are Large Shareholders Effective Monitors? An Investigation of Share Ownership and Corporate Performance in: Hubbard, R.G. (ed.), *Asymmetric Information, Corporate Finance and Investment*, Chicago, p.149-180.

ZERDICK, A., PICOT, A., SCHRAPE, K., ARTOPE, A., GOLDHAMMER, K., LANGE, U., VIERKANT, E., LOPEZ-ESCOBAR, E., SILVERSTONE, R.(2000), *E-Conomics, Strategies for the Digital Marketplace*, European Communication Council Report, Berlin.

ZINGALES, L. (2000), In Search of New Foundations, in: *Journal of Finance*, 55(4), p. 1623-1654.